교원임용시험 전공영어 대비 [제1판]

NEW

Build Up

박문각 임용
동영상강의 www.pmg.co.kr

KB213357

박현수 영어교육론

III-1 기출문제

Guideline for Pre-service Teachers
주제별 기출분석 정리

박문각

Preface

여러분이 보내고 있는 이 시간, 이 순간은 언젠가 교실 앞에 섰을 때, 누군가의 '처음'을 만들어주는 순간으로 이어질 것입니다. 우리가 배우는 수업 기법 하나, 말하기 활동 하나가 어떤 학생에게는 **영어에 대한 첫 인상**이자 영어를 사랑하게 되는 출발점이 될 수 있다고 믿습니다. 때로는 반복되는 공부에 지치고, 끝이 보이지 않을 때도 있지만 여러분의 한 걸음, 한 걸음은 분명히 **미래의 제자들의 삶**과 맞닿아 있을 것입니다.

전공영어의 수많은 이론들 속에 파묻힐 때마다, 문득 떠오르는 생각들.

"이 많은 이론들, 정말 교사가 된 후에도 쓸 수 있을까?"
"나는 지금 잘 가고 있는 걸까?"

그럴 때마다 스스로에게 되물어보세요. 학생 앞에 서서 처음으로 영어를 설명하게 될 때, 여러분이 건네는 한마디 한마디에 지금 이 순간의 고민과 공부가 고스란히 담긴다는 것을요. 영어교육론은 단지 시험을 위한 과목이 아니라 **교사로서의 시선과 수업을 바라보는 마음을 키워주는 길잡이**입니다. 우리가 읽고 외우는 이론 하나하나가 결국은 아이들의 눈을 반짝이게 할 수 있는 수업으로 연결될 수 있도록, 『Build-up III』는 단순한 기출문제 풀이를 넘어 교실 수업에 대한 이해와 공감, 그리고 수업을 상상하는 힘을 담고자 했습니다. 또한 실제 교실에서 적용 가능한 시각과 깊이 있는 이해를 쌓을 수 있도록 내용을 소주제로 나누어 구성하였습니다.

해마다 출제 경향은 조금씩 달라지지만, 결국 문제는 다음의 질문으로 귀결됩니다.

"진짜 교사가 되려는 사람이라면, 이 질문에 어떻게 답할까?"

그래서 『Build-up III』는 단순히 정답만을 제시하기보다, 문제 풀이의 사고 과정과 함께 해당 개념이 교실 수업 안에서 어떻게 적용되는지를 함께 숙고할 수 있도록 두 권으로 나누어 구성하였습니다.

Part I은 소주제에 따른 문항 분석과 대주제에 대한 Mapping을 통해 문제 풀이와 개념 정리를 함께 할 수 있도록 구성하였고, Part II는 학습 과제로서 동일 소주제에 대한 개별 문항 분석과 오답노트를 작성해 수험생 개개인의 주체적 문제 풀이 전략 수립과 점검이 가능하도록 설계하였습니다. 특히, 핵심 정보 찾기 연습을 통해 답안 작성의 실전 감각도 기를 수 있습니다.

오늘도 지친 몸을 이끌고 책상 앞에 앉아 있을 여러분을 생각하며, 한 페이지 한 페이지 마음을 담아 『Build-up Ⅲ』에 제 사랑을 엮었습니다. 쉬운 길이 아님을 알면서도 **교사의 길을 선택한 여러분의 그 마음이 참 고맙고 아름답습니다.**

교사들의 인권과 학교 현장의 여러 어려움에도 불구하고 당당히 그 길을 향해 걸어가는 여러분의 시작을 박현수, 그리고 『Build-up I, II, III』가 함께 할 수 있어 정말 기쁩니다.

수험의 길이 길고 지칠 수 있지만, 그 시간을 견디는 여러분은 분명 **누군가의 첫 번째 영어 선생님**이 되어 있을 것입니다. 그리고 여러분의 수업은 **누군가에게 배움의 시작**이 될 것입니다.

『Build-up I, II, III』, 그리고 앞으로 함께할 『Build-up IV』는 여러분의 합격은 물론, 그 이후 교사로서의 길까지 **따뜻한 응원과 동행**이 되기를 소망합니다.

이 책과 함께 한 뼘 더 성장할 여러분을 생각하며 2025년 4월의 봄날,

박현수

Guide

2025학년도 기출분석 및 2026학년도 대비 영어교육론 시험 전략

2025학년도 중등 임용시험의 영어교육론은 총 23문항 중 2024학년 기출 문항수(11문항)보다 한 문항 적은 10문항이 출제되어 총 80점 중 36점을 차지하였다. 여전히 교사 시험답게 영어교육론의 출제 비중이 50%에 달하는 것을 확인할 수 있다. 이것은 중등 임용시험의 정체성에 따라 영어교사의 필수 자질인 how to teach에 대한 자필평가의 중요성을 반영한 것으로 판단된다. 2025학년도 중등 임용시험은 전년도에 비해 비교적 난이도가 중/중하로 구성된 문항들이 출제되었으며, data-based item과 knowledge-based item이 기입형과 서술형에 고르게 출제되었다. 우선, 2025학년도 중등 임용 출제 방향을 살펴보면 첫째, 2022년 개정 교육과정의 주요 학습 개념인 Project-based learning과 digital literacy가 반영된 것을 확인할 수 있다. 둘째, 학생 중심 교실 수업을 계획할 수 있는 교사의 자질에 대한 평가로써 material adaptation, lesson objectives 및 modified lesson의 방식과 특징들이 출제되었다. 셋째, 학생 측면에서는 중간언어 형태의 특징과 reading strategies 등의 유무에 초점을 두어 출제되었으며, 마지막으로 언어학습의 최종 목표가 목표 문화의 수용이라는 측면에서 매년 문화지도가 출제되는 경향이 있는데 이번에도 역시 문화지도에 대한 내용이 출제되었다.

A형 기입형 문항

기입형 3, 4번은 예년보다는 평이한 개념이자 반복적으로 출제된 term인 'modifying'과 'inter-rater reliability'를 묻는 문항이 출제되었다. 이때 3번의 경우, term 도출 방식은 Original Material을 토대로 Adapted Material에 어떤 변화가 있는지 살펴보고, 해당 변화를 설명한 term을 data에서 고르는 방식으로 출제되었다. 4번의 term인 'inter-rater reliability'는 두 선생님의 대화 내용과 Mr. Lee의 Teaching Journal로 유추하여 찾을 수 있으며, comments에 나온 definition으로 해당 term을 확정할 수 있다. 다만, 4번은 data에서 찾아 쓰는 data-matching 방식으로 term을 도출했던 3번과 달리 example이나 situation, definition을 보고 해당 개념을 정확히 도출하는 knowledge-based 방식의 문항이다.

A형 서술형 문항

- 8번(data-based item)은 〈A〉에 학생들의 중간언어 발전 단계에 대한 L2 학생들의 다양한 변이적인 중간언어 형태에 관련된 설명과 예시를 data로 주고, 〈B〉에서 제공한 학생 대화와 matching하는 문항이다.
- 9번(data-based item)은 말하기 평가 원리에 관한 문항으로, 〈A〉에서 4개의 평가 원리를 제시하고 〈B〉에서 Mr. Jeong이 Item 1과 2에서 평가한 사례를 보고 matching하는 문항이다.
- 11번(knowledge-based item)은 〈A〉에서 각각 듣기/읽기와 말하기/쓰기에 대한 수업 목표를 제시하고, 〈B〉의 Teaching Procedure에서 제시되는 활동과의 관계를 파악하는 문항이다.
- 12번(data-based item)은 〈A〉에서 다양한 Reading Strategies에 대한 category를 제시하고 〈B〉에서 학생들의 읽기에 대한 문제점을 제공하여, 이를 해결할 수 있는 Reading Strategies를 고르는 문항이다.

B형 서술형 문항

- 6번(data-based item)은 〈A〉에 2022년 개정 교육과정의 핵심 교수 방법 중 하나인 Project-based learning에 대한 학습 단계가 제시되었고, 〈B〉에 실제 일정 기간(1st Week~6th Week)의 교실 수업 단계가 제시되어 두 단계 간의 mismatching을 묻는 문항이다.
- 7번(knowledge-based item)은 〈A〉에 제시된 초임교사와 주임교사 간 대화로 효율적인 수업을 위한 수업 계획 수정(modified lesson)에 관련된 문항으로, intensive listening을 이해하고 creative writing에 대한 개념을 묻는 문항이다.
- 10번(data-based item)은 다년간 중등 임용시험에서 주요 토픽으로 다루고 있는 문화학습 관련 문항이다. 〈A〉에서 문화학습 과정인 noticing, comparing, reflecting, interacting의 개념들과 두 학생의 문화학습 단계를 보여주는 발화 간 matching을 묻고 있고, 〈B〉에서는 두 학생의 대화로 알 수 있는 문화학습 과정을 규명하는 문항이다.
- 11번 문항(knowledge-based item)은 〈A〉에 how to use digital tools에 대한 원리를 제시하고, 〈B〉에서 8차 시간 수업 중 원리 mismatching에 대한 것을 고르는 문항이다. 이 문항은 discovery learning과 drill 간의 차이와 individualized feedback의 이해 여부를 묻는 문항이다.

2026학년도 대비 중등 임용 영어교육론의 방향

A형과 B형의 문항 유형에서 살펴봤듯이, 2025년 기출의 가장 큰 특징은 실제 교실 수업에서 교사의 자질과 학생들의 주도적 학습을 위한 교실 계획 및 언어학습의 궁극적인 목적인 목표 문화학습으로 꼽을 수 있다. 중등 임용시험에서 영어교육론의 난이도는 문학과 영어학 등 다른 영역에 비하면 중간 정도의 익숙한 문항들이 출제되고 있으나, 다른 내용학의 어려움에 대한 득점 손실을 만회할 수 있도록 영어교육론의 감점을 최소화하는 전략을 2026년 대비 중등 임용의 핵심 전략으로 삼아야 할 것이다. 이 목표를 성취하기 위해서는 영어교육론의 개념을 폭넓게 이해하고, 실전 문항의 data-processing / direction analysis/ correct answer에 대한 연습을 상반기부터 진행해야 한다.

Contents

Chapter 04 Classroom Assessment

Chapter 05 기출지문분석

NEW

Build Up

Chapter
01

Second Language Acquisition - Theoretical Background

Second Language Acquisition – Theoretical Background

1 Teaching Methods & Approaches

>> Possible Answers p.022

01 **Read the passages in <A> and <B>, and follow the directions.** [4 points]

2025 전공B 6번

A

Project-based learning (PBL) is a teaching method that facilitates students to use an inquiry process with an integrated goal and interrelated subsidiary tasks. One possible procedure for implementing PBL is provided below.

Students collaboratively set the goal and scope of the project. This makes students feel in control of their own projects from the beginning. Once the goal is set, students as a group actively discuss and decide upon what to include in their project. When collecting information for the project, students develop integrated language skills in meaningful ways. Students then create their projects collaboratively with their group members. Finally, students present their projects in class. When assessing student projects, the teacher evaluates students' learning progress, focusing on the process as well as the product.

B

Referring to the procedure as described in <A>, Ms. Park, a middle school English teacher, implemented PBL into her class over six weeks. Each week, one class session was allocated for the PBL project. When each session was over, Ms. Park briefly wrote a teacher's log to record events and observations. Some entries of her logs are provided below.

Week 1

I decided on a specific goal for the project and announced it to students. The goal was to make tourist brochures and distribute them to the local communities. I assigned students to groups of four. I also provided guidelines on the project.

Week 2

The groups explored possible destinations to include in their brochures. Students also searched the Internet for various brochures and analyzed the sections within. They found details including attractions, activities, and food.

Week 3

The groups conducted a survey on their classmates' recommendations for the destination their group decided upon. They did so by asking and responding to each other. Then they summarized the survey results.

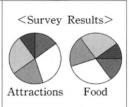

Week 4

The students worked closely in a group to make their brochures. Upon completion, they prepared for a group presentation.

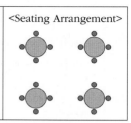

Week 5

Each group gave a ten-minute presentation. Students also prepared for distributing the brochures to the local communities.

Week 6

As the final step, I evaluated students' brochures based on a rubric, which consisted of vocabulary, grammar, and layout.

Identify the TWO weeks in <B> that do NOT follow the procedure provided in <A>. Then, explain how the identified weeks deviate from the procedure in <A>.

First Draft

Revised Version

02 Read the passage and follow the directions. [2 points] 2018 전공A 1번

Learning a second language (L2) may be viewed as the gradual transformation of performance from controlled to less controlled. This transformation has been called proceduralization or automatization and entails the conversion of declarative knowledge into procedural knowledge. According to this argument, the learning of skills is assumed to start with the explicit provision of relevant declarative knowledge and, through practice, this knowledge can hopefully convert into ability for use. At the same time, it is important to understand that learning an L2 may proceed in a different way. For example, some have wondered if incidental L2 learning is possible as a consequence of doing something else in the L2. Simply put, the question is about the possibility of learning without intention. The answer is still open, but, at present, it appears that people learn faster, more and better when they deliberately apply themselves to learning.

Read Mr. Lee's teaching log below and fill in the blank with the ONE most appropriate word from the passage above.

Through my teaching experience, I've learned that different students learn in different ways. Considering the current trend in teaching and learning, I believe that students should be provided with more opportunities to be exposed to the _____ learning condition. Minsu's case may illustrate that point. At the beginning of the semester, Minsu introduced himself as a book lover. He wanted to read novels in English but was not sure if he could. I suggested that he didn't have to try to comprehend all the details. Indeed, Minsu has benefitted a lot from reading novels. He said he learned many words and expressions even though he did not make attempts to memorize them. I will continue observing his progress as his way of learning is of great interest.

Your Answer _____

03 **Read the dialogue and follow the directions.** [2 points] 2018 전공A 3번

> T1：There's no doubt that young children beginning school need the basics of reading, writing, and math.
>
> T2：I agree, but the big problem is determining the best way for them to get it. I think the classic mode of a teacher at the chalkboard, and books and homework is outdated.
>
> T1：True. That's why I have been looking at some teaching literature based on the ideas Jonathan Bergman and Aaron Sams came up with.
>
> T2：What do they suggest?
>
> T1：Well, they have reconsidered the role of the traditional classroom and home. So home becomes a classroom, and vice versa in this way of learning. Students view lecture materials, usually in the form of videos, as homework before class.
>
> T2：That's interesting. What's the focus in class?
>
> T1：That's the best part. Class time is reserved for activities such as interactive discussions or collaborative work supervised by the teacher.
>
> T2：I like it. But how does it benefit the students?
>
> T1：They can study the lectures at home at their own pace, or re-watch the videos, if needed, or even skip parts they already understand.
>
> T2：Right. And then, in class the teacher is present when they apply new knowledge. What about traditional homework?
>
> T1：That can be done in class, too. So, the teacher can gain insights into whatever concepts, if any, their students are struggling with and adjust the class accordingly.
>
> T2：What does the literature say about its effectiveness?
>
> T1：Amazingly, according to one study, 71% of teachers who have tried this approach in their classes noticed improved grades, and 80% reported improved student attitudes, as well.
>
> T2：That's fantastic. Let me read that when you're done. I want to look further into this.
>
> T=teacher

01

Fill in the blank with the ONE most appropriate word.

> The teaching approach discussed by the two teachers is known technically
> as _____ learning in educational settings.

Your Answer _____

04 **Read the passage in <A> and the examples in <B>, and follow the directions.** [4 points] 2022 전공B 11번

A

Focus on form is one of the approaches to L2 instruction that has been proposed to develop learners' fluency and accuracy. It occurs when learners briefly pay attention to linguistic items within a larger meaning-focused context. Focus on form can be accomplished in various ways. A basic distinction is drawn between 'reactive focus on form' (where attention to form arises out of some problem in a participant's production as in A1 and A2 below) and 'pre-emptive focus on form' (where the participants make a particular form the topic of the conversation even though no actual problem has arisen as in B1 and B2 below).

	Options	Description
Reactive	A1. Implicit feedback	The teacher or another student responds to a student's error without directly indicating an error has been made, e.g., by means of a recast or a clarification request.
	A2. Explicit feedback	The teacher or another student responds to a student's error by directly indicating that an error has been made, e.g., by formally correcting the error or by using metalanguage.
Pre-emptive	B1. Student-initiated focus on form	A student asks a question about a linguistic form.
	B2. Teacher-initiated focus on form	The teacher gives advice about a linguistic form he/she thinks might be problematic or asks the students a question about the form.

01

B

Example 1

(It is Monday morning and a group of students have just arrived for their English class. The teacher starts the class by asking the students about their weekend.)

T : So what did you do this weekend?

S1 : I ran my first marathon!

T : Wow! Did you finish?

S1 : Yes, eventually.... It was actually a half-course marathon, but really challenging.

T : Way to go! *(turning to S2)* How about you?

S2 : I had gone to the park...

T : You need to use the past simple when you say the things you did over the weekend.

S2 : I has b..., I had?

T : Past simple. For example, I saw, I did, or I played ...

S2 : Ah! I went to the park with my family last weekend.

T : Great! How was it? Did you and your family enjoy it?

S2 : Very much.

Example 2

(Students are doing a communicative task with their conversation partner in their English class. The students are asked to set a date when they can do a project together. While students are checking the date, the teacher shuttles back and forth among the groups.)

S1 : Teacher, is it okay to just say December eighteen?

T : December eighteen?

S1 : Yeah, like December eighteen or January seventeen.

S2 : You know, we need to fix the date we meet together, and we want to make sure the right way of saying dates.

T : Mmm. It's okay but it sounds a little casual. Usually December THE eighteen*th* or THE eighteen*th* of December.

S1 : Aha! December THE eighteen*th*.

T : Yeah, good.

T=teacher, S=student

Among the options A1, A2, B1, and B2 in <A>, identify the option of focus on form used in each example in <B>, respectively. Then, support your answers with evidence from <B>.

First Draft

_____

_____

_____

_____

_____

_____

_____

_____

Revised Version

_____

_____

_____

_____

_____

_____

_____

Create a semantic map of teaching methods & approaches based on your understanding.

Possible Answers

01 Week 1 and Week 6 do not align with the PBL procedure. In Week 1, Ms. Park directly sets and announces the project goal to the students, instead of allowing them to collaboratively determine the goal and scope of the project. In Week 6, she evaluates students' learning progress based solely on the final products—brochures—without assessing both the learning process and the product.

02 incidental

03 flipped

04 Example 1 represents Option A2 since the teacher gives explicit feedback on S2's error saying "You need to use past simple" with metalanguage. On the other hand, Example 2 shows Option B1 in that S1 asks a question about how to say dates before an actual problem occurs.

2 Interlanguage Development

>> Possible Answers p.030

01 **Read the passage in <A> and the conversation in <B>, and follow the directions.** [4 points] 2025 전공A 8번

A

Understanding second language (L2) learners' interlanguage is an important step for teaching L2 learners. In analyzing interlanguage, it has been found that deviations from characteristics of the target language exist in learners' utterances. For example, deviations in early L2 learners' utterances can be categorized into several types.

<Deviations in Early L2 Learners' Utterances>

Type	Description	Example (The intended meaning is in parentheses.)
Mismatched lexical class	The lexical class does not match.	*It's a pink.* (It's pink.)
Semantic deviation	Utterances are semantically ill-formed.	*What's the spaghetti?* (Do you like spaghetti?)
Number of arguments	Utterances contain more or fewer arguments than required.	*I wore.* (I wore a shirt.)
Word order	Word order is violated.	*I this book read.* (I read this book.)
...	...	...

B

(Two students are carrying out a two-way spot-the-difference task in their English class.)

S1: Now, let's get started. In your picture, are there chairs?

S2: Yes.

S1: How many chairs are there?

S2: Two chairs.

S1: There are also two chairs in my picture. Now, please ask me about my picture.

S2: What's the pen?

S1: I'm sorry? Do you mean, "Do you have a pen?"

S2: Yes.

S1: Okay. Then, yes, I do. Do you have a pen?

S2: No, I do not have a pen.

S1: Okay. Then we've found one difference. Next, your turn.

S2: Is there a girl?

S1: Yes, there is. What is she doing?

S2: She is giving Mary.

S1: Um, what is she giving Mary?

S2: Ah, she is giving Mary a book.

S1: Oh, in my picture, she is giving Mary an eraser.

S2: Yeah! Finally, we got them all.

S=student

Based on <A>, identify the TWO types of deviations found in the students' utterances in <B>. Then, explain your answers, respectively, with evidence from <B>.

First Draft

_____
_____
_____
_____
_____
_____
_____
_____

Revised Version

_____
_____
_____
_____
_____
_____
_____
_____

02 Read the passage in <A> and the conversation in <B>, and follow the directions. [4 points] 2023 전공A 10번

A

    Second language learners pass through a predictable sequence of development. Since the early 1990's, some research has investigated the acquisition of pragmatic abilities in the L2. 'Requesting' is one of the pragmatic features that has received attention. In a review of studies on the acquisition of requests in English, six stages of development were suggested.

Stage	Characteristics	Example
1	Using body language or gestures	*Sir (pointing to the pencil).* *Teacher (holding the paper).*
2	Using verbless expressions	*A paper. / More time.*
3	Using imperative verbs	*Give me. / Give me a paper.*
4	Using 'Can I have _____?' as a formulaic expression	*Can I have some candy?*
5	Using 'can' with a range of verbs, not just with 'have'	*Can you pass me the book?*
6	Using indirect requests	*I want more cookies.*

B

(Students are doing a problem-solving task in groups. S1 plays the role of moderator in the activity.)

S1 : We have to find some ways to make the environment more sustainable. Suhee, what's your opinion?

S2 : I'm sorry, but nothing comes to mind now. I need more time to think.

S1 : Okay. Tell us if you're ready. Minho, how about you? Can you share your ideas with us?

S3 : We should use one-time products as less as possible.

S1 : Hold on, Minho. What does 'one-time products' mean? Can I have some examples?

S3 : Well, paper cups, plastic bags...

S2 : Ah, I see. You mean 'disposable products', right?

S3 : Yes.

S1 : Minho, I like your idea.

S2 : I'm ready. Driving electronic cars reduces air pollution.

S3 : Sounds great.

S1 : Now I think we have enough opinions for the presentation. Suhee, can you speak for us in the presentation session?

S2 : I'm afraid not. Minho can do better than me.

S3 : Umm. Okay. I'll take the speaker role. I'll do my best.

S2 : Thanks, Minho. I'll write the presentation script for you.

S1 : Wow, thank you.

S=student

Based on <A>, identify the developmental stages where S1 and S2 are, respectively. Then, explain your answers with evidence from <B>.

First Draft

_____
_____
_____
_____
_____
_____
_____
_____

Revised Version

_____
_____
_____
_____
_____
_____
_____

Create a semantic map of interlanguage development based on your understanding.

Self Mapping

Possible Answers

01   In the conversation, S2 demonstrates 'Semantic deviation' and a deviation in the 'Number of arguments'. First, S2 produces the ill-formed utterance, 'What's the pen?' instead of the intended meaning, "Do you have a pen?". Additionally, S2 says "She is giving Mary," where the necessary argument, 'a book' is omitted.

02   While S1 belongs to Stage 5, S2 is at Stage 6 in terms of developmental stage. S1 uses 'can' with various verbs such as 'share' or 'speak' for requests. On the other hand, S2 uses indirect requests like "I need more time to think." (or "Minho can do better than me.")

3 Learning Phenomenon

>> Possible Answers p.036

01 **Read the conversation and follow the directions.** [2 points] 2023 전공A 1번

(Ms. Kim, a new teacher, and Mr. Song, a head teacher, are discussing Ms. Kim's concerns about her student's writing performance.)

T1 : Ms. Kim, did the process-oriented evaluation in your writing class go well this semester?

T2 : I'm still making comments to students, but there is something I'm worried about.

T1 : What is it?

T2 : I'm afraid that one of my students is making more errors now than he was at the beginning of the semester.

T1 : He got worse as the semester went on?

T2 : Yes. He turned in the writing assignment. However, there were so many errors in his writing.

T1 : What kinds of errors?

T2 : Unlike the beginning of the semester, now he has problems with irregular verbs.

T1 : Can you give me an example?

T2 : When the semester began, he wrote words like "drank," "wore," and "heard" without errors. Now I am seeing errors like "drinked," "weared," and "heared." He is suddenly treating irregular verbs like regular verbs.

T1 : Hmm. Now that I think about it, he is probably progressing!

T2 : What are you talking about?

T1 : Well, according to U-shaped course of development, he is starting to understand the rules of the past tense.

T2 : Oh, I see.

T1=Mr. Song, T2=Ms. Kim

Fill in the blank with the ONE most appropriate word.

In the above conversation, Ms. Kim's student seems to regress, making errors with irregular verbs that he used to use correctly, due to overgeneralization. This phenomenon is commonly called _____, in which the learner seems to have grasped a rule or principle but then moves from a correct form to an incorrect form.

Your Answer _____

02 **Read the passage in <A> and the teacher's log in <B>, and follow the directions.** [4 points] 2019 전공A 11번

| A |

Language transfer refers to the effects of the learner's previous language knowledge or performance on subsequent language learning. Transfer can be categorized into positive and negative transfer. Negative transfer can be further divided into two types overgeneralization and interference.

| B |

(Following is a teacher's reflection on a task for her Korean students.)

Teacher's log

I conducted a task that required students in pairs to ask and answer questions in class yesterday. At the beginning of the task, I heard a student asking, "Don't you like bananas?" His partner answered, "No, I eat them everyday. They are good for my health." And another student said, "Yes, I never eat them. But I like mangos," when responding to "Don't you like oranges?" I noticed many other students make such errors later in the course of the task. So I decided to tap into the errors and explained them to students after the task. I gave them further question-and-answer exercises to provide opportunities to practice what I explained before the class was over.

Identify the type of negative transfer in <B> based on <A>. Then, provide TWO examples of the identified type from <B> and explain why they exemplify the identified type in terms of whether transfer occurs intralingually or interlingually.

First Draft

_____

_____

_____

_____

_____

_____

_____

_____

Revised Version

_____

_____

_____

_____

_____

_____

_____

_____

Create a semantic map of learning phenomenon based on your understanding.

Self
Mapping

Possible Answers

01   backsliding

02   The type of negative transfer in ⟨B⟩ is 'interference,' which occurs interlingually. Korean students incorrectly apply L1 rules for answering negative questions in English. For example, Korean students respond to the negative questions like "Don't you like bananas?" and "Don't you like oranges?" as follows: "No, I eat them everyday." and "Yes, I never eat them."

4 Discourse Structures & Negotiation Strategies

>> Possible Answers p.044

01 **Read the teacher's journal and follow the directions.** [2 points] 2024 전공B 1번

Teacher's Journal

Speech acts are a minimum unit of communication, which I believe are an important aspect of the pragmatic knowledge L2 learners need to learn to avoid unsuccessful communication. My students, for instance, have shown quite a few communication failures over time. When I tried to find out what their failures have in common, I realized they did not recognize the fact that an utterance may have some hidden intended effects on the hearer. Indeed, our communication is _____ in nature in that when we are saying something, we can mean something else.

I recall a couple of examples in particular. One day, in class, I said to my student, "What a wonderful picture you have drawn! I really like it." The student responded, "Oh, you like it? You can have it." In this case, since I made a compliment, I expected a simple thank-you from the student. Beyond my expectation, he seemed to believe that I wanted to own his picture. In a poetry class, I once said to another student of mine, "Would you like to read the poem?" The student replied, "No, I wouldn't." In the second case, I made a request, but the student seemed to think I was asking her to tell me if she was willing or unwilling to read the poem. In both cases, it is apparent that my students misunderstood the _____ acts my utterances performed.

Fill in the blanks with the ONE most appropriate word. Use the SAME word in both blanks.

(Your Answer) _____

02 **Read the passage in <A> and the conversation in <B>, and follow the directions.** [4 points] 2022 전공B 6번

A

Conversation is co-constructed by two or more people, unfolding dynamically in real time. For conversational discourse to be successful, the participants have to know how to organize the events in it; that is, they need to achieve cohesion. A cohesive relation is one in which the interpretation of one element in the discourse presupposes, and is dependent upon, another. In English, along with the grammatical cohesive devices such as reference, substitution, ellipsis, and conjunction, cohesion in conversation can also be achieved using lexical cohesive devices.

Lexical cohesive devices by which links are made across a conversation include the use of synonyms, antonyms, repetition of the same content words, words exhibiting general-specific relations, and words displaying part-whole relations. The use of lexical cohesion is an indicator of topic consistency, and hence contributes significantly to the sense that speakers are talking to topic, and the talk, therefore, becomes more coherent.

B

(Two friends are having a conversation in the wallpaper aisle at a hardware store.)

S1 : Isn't it funny that wallpaper is in fashion again?

S2 : Yeah, I thought it was gone forever.

S1 : Me, too. So, you are redoing your kitchen?

S2 : Yup. And I want to use one of these.

S1 : Good idea. *(pointing to a roll of wallpaper)* How about that?

S2 : You mean the one on the top shelf?r

S1 : Yeah, do you like it?

S2 : Uh-huh. It will go with my dining table.

S1 : Have you been to Lesley's new office?

S2 : I have, actually. It was huge and everything was so well organized.

S1 : Yeah. And she had the same wallpaper.

S2 : Oh, that's right. I remember that.

S=speaker

01

Based on <A>, identify TWO lexical cohesive devices used in the conversation in <B>. Then, provide evidence from <B> for each identified lexical cohesive device.

First Draft

_____

_____

_____

_____

_____

_____

_____

Revised Version

_____

_____

_____

_____

_____

_____

_____

03 **Read the passage in <A> and the interaction in <B>, and follow the directions.** [4 points] 2020 전공B 4번

A

   When problems in conveying meaning occur in conversational interactions, interlocutors need to interrupt the flow and negotiate meaning in order to overcome communication breakdowns and to understand what the conversation is about. A negotiation routine may have a sequence of four components:

- A *trigger* is an utterance that causes communication difficulty.
- An *indicator* alerts the speaker of the trigger that a problem exists.
- A *response* is the component through which the speaker of the trigger attempts to resolve the communication difficulty.
- A *reaction to response* can tell the speaker of the trigger whether or not the problem has been resolved.

B

(The following is a student-student talk occurring in the morning.)

S1: You didn't come to the baseball practice yesterday. What happened?
S2: Nothing serious. I had to study for an exam.
S1: I am sorry you missed the practice. Have you taken the exam yet?
S2: Yes. I took it a little while ago.
S1: How did you do?
S2: Hopefully I did OK. I didn't get any sleep last night.
S1: I guess you must be drained.
S2: Drained? What do you mean?
S1: It's similar to 'tired.'
S2: Oh, I see. Yeah, I am very tired.
S1: You need to take a break.
S2: I sure do, but I think I am going to eat something first.

                                                                    S=student

Identify an utterance from <B> that is a *response* mentioned in <A>, and explain how the speaker attempts to resolve the communication difficulty with the identified utterance. Then, identify an utterance from <B> that is a *reaction to response* mentioned in <A>, and explain whether the communication difficulty is resolved with the identified utterance.

First Draft

_____

_____

_____

_____

_____

_____

_____

Revised Version

_____

_____

_____

_____

_____

_____

_____

04 Read the online discussion about Hyun's opinion and fill in the blank with TWO words from the passage. [2 points] 2016 전공A 7번

Hyun
As an international language, English has many varieties used and taught around the world. Have you ever thought about English varieties?

📝 like it 28 | recommend it 15

Sarah
Yes! There are many varieties of English. Americans, Australians, Brits and Canadians have many variations in how they use English. Naturally, this exists between non-native speakers, too. I think we should be aware of this reality. Many English teachers in the world today are non-native speakers of English. We need to consider this issue for teacher training and language instruction.

Bill
I agree. Although I am a native English teacher, like many of you, we need to recognize the validity of a variety of Englishes, or better known as, _____ . These include established outer-circle varieties such as Indian English, Singaporean English, and Nigerian English.

Min
Perhaps, but what about standardization? Shouldn't we focus on one clearly understood form of the language for consistency and intelligibility?

Jun
I don't think that is applicable in all cases, Min. The needs and attitudes of students, teachers, and administrators have an influence on the norm or standard adopted for instruction; it is thus best that local norms be respected whenever possible.

Your Answer _____

Create a semantic map of discourse structures & negotiation strategies based on your understanding.

Self
Mapping

Possible Answers

01   illocutionary

02   Two lexical cohesive devices used in ⟨B⟩ are repetition of the same content words and words displaying part—whole relations. The word "wallpaper" is repeated multiple times by both speakers. Also, "kitchen" and "dining table" show a part—whole relation.

03   The response is "It's similar to 'tired.'" S1 explains the word "drained" by providing an easy synonym, "tired," as a form of lexical modification. Also, the reaction to response is "Oh, I see. Yeah, I am very tired." This shows that S2 understands the meaning.

04   World Englishes

5 Cultural Learning

>> Possible Answers p.054

01 Read the passage in <A> and the conversation in <B>, and follow the directions. [4 points] 2025 전공B 10번

A

Intercultural language learning in the classroom can be conceptualized as a series of four interrelated processes: *noticing, comparing, reflecting,* and *interacting*. First, noticing is for learners to experience new input about culture and attempt to understand it. Teachers may use various exemplifications of the target culture as input, such as videos, written texts, and cartoons. Second, comparing occurs when learners are engaged in identifying similarities and differences between learners' culture and the target culture. Third, reflecting implies that learners make personal interpretations of experiences and react to linguistic and cultural diversity. Finally, interacting involves learners communicating personal meanings about their experiences, exploring those meanings, and reshaping them in response to others.

The two excerpts below are parts of students' speeches in class.

Excerpt from Seoyeon's Speech

"I imagined what I would and wouldn't like about attending a U.S. high school. I'd be excited about having many options for extracurricular activities, but I wouldn't want to join any sport teams because I don't like playing sports."

Excerpt from Taesoo's Speech

"I think the level of engagement in extracurricular activities seems different between Korean and U.S. high school students. For example, many U.S. high school students tend to spend much more time doing community service than Korean students."

As seen above, Seoyeon is most likely involved in the process of ① _____, and Taesoo is most likely involved in the process of ② _____.

B

(Seoyeon and Taesoo are talking about their speeches.)

Seoyeon : I really liked your speech. There are a lot of things we can do for the community when it comes to extracurricular activities.

Taesoo : Thank you. That was the exact point I wanted to make.

Seoyeon : I'd like to hear more about the ways in which we can serve our communities.

Fill in the blanks ① and ② each with the ONE most appropriate word from <A>, in the correct order. Then, explain one of the four processes in <A> that Seoyeon in <B> is most likely involved in with evidence from <B>.

First Draft

Revised Version

02 **Read the passages in <A> and <B>, and follow the directions.** [4 points]

A

    This semester, Ms. Kang, a high school English teacher, has been assigned to teach a new elective course called the 'Culture of English Speaking Countries.' The goal of the course is to help students develop intercultural competence. She consulted multiple resources including the national curriculum, books, and her colleagues from other schools who have taught similar courses in order to achieve the course goal. Based on her research, she has come up with the teaching plan presented below.

A Teaching Plan for 'Culture of English Speaking Countries'

1. Teaching Contents

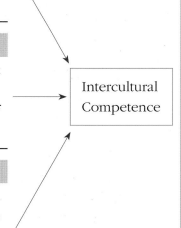

Cultural Products
tangible and intangible creations produced or adopted by the members of the culture (e.g., tools, clothing, music, spoken language, etc.)

Cultural Practices
actions and interactions carried out by the members of the culture (e.g., greetings, being punctual, ways of interacting with elders, etc.)

Cultural Perspectives
perceptions, values, beliefs, and attitudes held by the members of the culture (e.g., religious beliefs, attitudes towards authority figures, etc.)

Intercultural Competence

---

2. Teaching Principles
   1) Integrate language skills and culture.
   2) Utilize different types of audiovisual aids.
   3) Avoid reinforcing associations between nationalities(countries) and cultures.
   4) Involve students in discovering English culture, instead of transmitting information.
   5) Assess students' achievements based on their performances at the end of the lesson.

B

Below is one of the lesson sequences that Ms. Kang has developed to implement her teaching plan.

Lesson Sequence

1. Preparation: Assemble a selection of pictures illustrating a variety of British and American dwellings.
2. In Class:
   1) Write the word 'Houses' on the board, and ask students about the common housing styles in their local community.
   2) Show pictures of houses on the screen with their names one by one (e.g., ranch houses, cottages, brownstones, semi-detached houses, terraced houses, bungalows, duplexes, townhouses, etc.) and read the names with students.
   3) Play a video of two people talking in English about typical British and American housing styles and then check students' comprehension.
   4) Hand out a worksheet with the pictures and the names of houses. Have students classify the houses into two groups and write their names in the correct column. Check the answers together.

Houses in the UK	Houses in the US
e.g., semi-detached houses	e.g., ranch houses

5) Divide students into groups of three. Have each group choose one house type and research online the types of materials used in the house, its layout, the characteristics of the rooms, walls, gardens, etc.

6) Have each group give a short presentation in English about the house type they researched. Assess them using a scoring rubric.

Based on <A>, identify the ONE teaching content that Ms. Kang incorporates and the ONE teaching principle that she does NOT conform to in her lesson sequence in <B>. Then explain your answers with evidence from <A> and <B>.

First Draft

_____

_____

_____

_____

_____

_____

_____

Revised Version

_____

_____

_____

_____

_____

_____

_____

03 **Read the passage in <A> and the scenarios in <B>, and follow the directions.** [4 points] 2022 전공A 10번

| A |

In most intercultural conflict situations, interactants are expected to defend or save their faces when they are threatened. Here, face refers to a person's sense of favorable self-worth or self-image experienced in communication. The various ways to deal with conflict and face are called facework or facework strategies. There are three general types of facework strategies used in intercultural conflict. Below are the three types and the specific behaviors displayed when employing a strategy.

Facework Strategies	Facework Behaviors
A. Dominating: an effort to control the conflict situation	A1. Assault the other verbally
	A2. Be firm in one's demands and do not give in
B. Avoiding: an attempt to save the other person's face	B1. Dismiss the conflict that threatens the other's face
	B2. Rely on a third party to manage the conflict
C. Integrating: an endeavor for closure of the conflict	C1. Offer an apology for the conflict
	C2. Mutually acknowledge each other's good points

B

Scenario 1

Michael and Ken are students from different countries taking the same class at an Australian university. They are partners for an assignment and decide to meet twice a week. However, Michael is always late for the meetings. Ken feels frustrated because in his culture, punctuality is highly important and making others wait is regarded inconsiderate. Ken finally tells Michael how he feels. Hearing Ken's complaints, Michael is upset at first. He thinks Ken is fussing over nothing because in Michael's culture, people are more flexible with time. After consideration, he comes to understand Ken's position and admits his fault. Then, expressing his regret, he promises to be on time.

Scenario 2

Maria and Sue are students rooming together at a US university. They are from different countries. Maria loves hanging out with her friends and invites them to the room to talk and eat. They almost always leave after midnight. However, Sue is irritated because in her culture, staying late at someone's place is not normally acceptable. In contrast, Maria doesn't mind her friends staying late since in her culture, getting along well with other people is a high priority. Sue considers directly telling Maria that her friends should not outstay their welcome. Not wanting to create an unpleasant situation, however, she instead decides to go to the library when her roommate's friends visit.

Based on <A>, identify ONE facework behavior that Michael and Sue each display to deal with their intercultural conflicts in <B>, respectively. Then, explain your answers with evidence from <B>.

First Draft

_____

_____

_____

_____

_____

_____

_____

Revised Version

_____

_____

_____

_____

_____

_____

_____

Create a semantic map of cultural learning based on your understanding.

Possible Answers

01 ① reflecting ② comparing

Seoyeon in ⟨B⟩ engages in the process of interacting as she shares her personal meanings after learning about extracurricular activities in the U.S. and reshapes her understanding of extracurricular activities to include diverse ways to provide community services through her interaction with Taesoo.

02 Ms. Kang incorporates Cultural Products as teaching content by introducing a variety of British and American houses as tangible creations. However, she reinforces the association between nationalities and cultures by having students classify the housing styles into two countries, the UK and the US, which goes against Principle (3).

03 Michael displays C1, while Sue shows B1. After realizing the cultural difference, Michael apologizes by admitting his fault and promising to be on time. As for Sue, instead of confronting Maria directly, she avoids a face-threatening conflict by choosing to go to the library.

Create a semantic map of theoretical background based on your understanding.

Self
Mapping

NEW
Build Up

Chapter

02

Classroom Contexts

Classroom Contexts

1 Learner Variables

≫ Possible Answers p.066

01 **Read the passage in <A> and the dialogue in <B>, and follow the directions.** [4 points] 2022 전공A 9번

A

While styles are preferred ways of processing information, strategies are conscious mental and behavioural procedures that people engage in with the aim to gain control over their learning process. Although the definitions and boundaries of learning strategies can be varied, there are several categories of strategies that have generally been agreed upon, as shown below.

Strategy	Definition	Examples
Metacognitive	Learners being consciously aware of their thought processes and cognition	• Planning • Monitoring • Evaluating
Cognitive	Learners using their brains to manipulate or transform L2 input in order to retain it	• Keyword technique • Repetition • Inferencing • Visualization
Social	Learners involving others in their L2 learning processes	• Having conversations in L2 with other speakers • Practicing L2 with other classmates
Affective	Learners engaging their own emotions to facilitate L2 learning	• Rewarding oneself for studying • Intentionally reducing anxiety

B

Mina : Hi, Junho. Is everything going well?

Junho : Hey, Mina! Good to see you here. Can I ask you something?

Mina : Sure. What's up?

Junho : I know you are a good English learner and I'd like to get some tips.

Mina : Sure. Will you tell me how you study?

Junho : I try to set schedules for learning. For example, I decide what I should study first and what I can study at a later time.

Mina : That's a good way. Anything else you do?

Junho : While studying, I sometimes stop to check my comprehension.

Mina : Okay. In my case, I usually create pictures in my mind to remember the things I've studied.

Junho : Oh, you do? I've never tried to create mental images when I study.

Mina : Actually, it helps me remember things a lot longer.

Junho : That makes sense. I think I need to try it.

Mina : And, whenever I find some difficult English expressions I'm not familiar with, I talk in English with native speakers to find out exactly what those expressions mean.

Junho : I usually use my online dictionary. But I often find the dictionary explanation is rather difficult for me.

Mina : That happens a lot. I think asking questions to others is one of the best ways to clarify the meaning.

Junho : I quite agree. I'll apply your advice to my English learning immediately. Thanks for your tips!

Identify TWO strategies in <A> that Mina recommended to Junho in <B>. Then, support your answers with evidence from <B>.

First Draft

_____

_____

_____

_____

_____

_____

_____

Revised Version

_____

_____

_____

_____

_____

_____

_____

02 Read the lesson procedure and follow the directions. [2 points] 2016 전공A 1번

Lesson Procedure

1. Ss listen to a recorded conversation about the topic of the lesson.
2. T asks Ss to make associations among key words and to guess the meaning of the words from context. Then T teaches new vocabulary.
3. Ss read passages and find semantic clues to get the main idea.
4. Ss reread the passages and scan for specific information.
5. Ss, in groups, do categorizing activities.
6. Ss discuss the topic and write a short comment on it.
7. T hands out the checklist and has Ss keep a daily log after school for one week.

A Daily Learning Log

Name: **Jihae Park**

※ Respond to each of the following statements with a checkmark (✔).

	Day 1			Day 2			Day 3			Day 4			Day 5		
	1	2	3	1	2	3	1	2	3	1	2	3	1	2	3
1. I make guesses to understand unfamiliar words.															
2. I first read over passages quickly, and then go back and reread them.															
3. I make summaries of the text that I read in English.															
19. I ask a friend questions about schoolwork.															
20. I write down my feelings in a language learning diary.															

Note: 1 = Never, 2 = Sometimes, 3 = Always

T=teacher, S=student

Complete the comments by filling in the blanks with the SAME word.

> The lesson procedure shows that the students are instructed to practice various kinds of _____ during the class. Also, they are encouraged to be aware of their use of _____ by keeping a daily learning log.

Your Answer _____

03 Read the passage in <A> and the conversation in <B>, and follow the directions. [5 points] 2015 전공A 서술형 2번

A

In negotiation of meaning, "uptake" refers to an interlocutor's immediate response to his or her partner's signal of noncomprehension. In uptake, the interlocutor often uses a variety of communication strategies such as message abandonment, topic change, circumlocution, word coinage, foreignizing, and code switching.

B

The following is part of a teacher-student interaction that contains negotiation of meaning.

T : Hi, Sangjee. How was your weekend?

S : Hello. Well, I had a busy weekend.

T : Did you go anywhere?

S : No, I stayed home all weekend.

T : Why were you busy, then?

S : I had to fly ten chickens.

T : Uh, what? What did you do?

S : Uh, you know, put chickens in oil, very hot oil, kind of bake them.

T : Oh, you FRIED them!

S : Yeah, I fried them with my mother.

T : Why did you have to fry that many chickens?

S : We had a big party on Sunday. My grandfather's birthday. Many people came.

T : Oh, so that's why you fried so many. The party must have been a lot of fun.

T=teacher, S=student

Identify where the uptake takes place by writing the specific utterance from <B>, and select the strategy used in the uptake from those in <A>. Then explain how the utterance in the uptake shows the selected strategy.

First Draft _____

_____

_____

_____

_____

_____

_____

_____

Revised Version _____

_____

_____

_____

_____

_____

_____

_____

_____

Create a semantic map of learner variables based on your understanding.

Self
Mapping

Possible Answers

01 Mina recommends each of cognitive and social strategies to Junho. First, she advises him to visualize what he has studied in his mind. Second, she suggests talking with native English speakers to figure out the exact meaning whenever he encounters a difficult expression.

02 strategies

03 The uptake occurs in the student's fourth utterance when the student says "put chickens in oil, very hot oil, kind of bake them." This shows circumlocution as a communication strategy, as the student explains the unfamiliar word "fry" by describing the cooking process instead of naming it directly.

2 Classroom Management

>> Possible Answers p.089

01 Read the passage in <A> and a teacher's note in <B>, and follow the directions. [2 points] 2020 전공A 2번

A

Curriculum design is a series of systematic efforts to develop a curriculum that satisfies the target learners as well as teachers. Researchers suggest that there are five main stages in the process of designing a curriculum.

```
┌─────────────────────────────┐
│     _____      │
└─────────────────────────────┘
              ⇓
┌─────────────────────────────┐
│      Goal Specifications     │
└─────────────────────────────┘
              ⇓
┌─────────────────────────────┐
│    Materials Development     │
└─────────────────────────────┘
              ⇓
┌─────────────────────────────┐
│  Language Teaching & Learning │
└─────────────────────────────┘
              ⇓
┌─────────────────────────────┐
│    Curriculum Evaluation     │
└─────────────────────────────┘
```

B

Teacher's Note

    I am planning to develop a new English course for winter session, so I wanted to establish the basis for developing the curriculum. The first step of this process requires me to systematically collect and analyze areas of necessity for my students in order to satisfy their language learning requirements. So, I created a survey which asked students questions about their English deficiencies and the difficulties they face in performing certain language tasks in their current classes. It also asked them about the methods they enjoy learning through as well as the types of English skills that they want to improve. For the second step of this process, I wanted to get more information about the students' preferred learning styles and interests, so I referred to my classroom observation notes to learn about them. I then asked my school's principal to show me the results of their placement tests to gain an understanding of their levels of linguistic proficiency and background experience. Furthermore, I interviewed students both in groups and individually to get more detailed information. In short, I conducted _____ by collecting all these data.

Based on the information in <A> and <B>, fill in the blanks in <A> and <B> with the TWO most appropriate words. Use the SAME words in both blanks.

Your Answer   _____

02 **Read the conversation in <A> and the draft of the syllabus in <B>, and follow the directions.** [4 points] 2024 전공A 11번

A

T1 : Mr. Choi, can we talk about a syllabus for the Business English course next semester? We need to develop one as soon as possible.

T2 : Sure. What type of syllabus do you have in mind?

T1 : Well, I think a multi-layered syllabus would be most appropriate.

T2 : I agree. I'd like to cover various aspects of Business English, such as topics, functions, skills, activities, grammar, and vocabulary.

T1 : Sounds good to me. First of all, I believe all the topics should be business-related. But what about the functions? Do you have anything in mind?

T2 : I think we should teach functions that are often used in business situations.

T1 : Yes. By doing so, we'll prepare the students to perform well when they get a job.

T2 : We also have to make sure that both receptive and productive skills are included.

T1 : Definitely. We should provide activities where students can practice both skills.

T2 : Okay. How about grammar? I think our students are not good at making connections between ideas, so we need to incorporate connective devices in the syllabus as well.

T1 : Good. We also need to make sure there is a vocabulary component, right?

T2 : Of course. You know, English courses in our school tend to focus on single words but not multi-word units like collocations, idioms, and fixed expressions.

T1 : You're right. If we teach those multi-word units during the course, students will be able to speak more fluently.

T2 : Great! Based on what we've discussed so far, I'll write a draft. Can you check it later?

T1 : Sure. I look forward to seeing it completed.

T=teacher

B

This is the draft of the syllabus T2 wrote.

Components	Unit 1	Unit 2	Unit 3
Topics	• Business Relations	• Business Negotiation	• Business Meetings
Functions	• Greeting and introducing in work places • Receiving buyers	• Making business contracts • Dealing with orders	• Planning business meetings • Attending business meetings
Skills	• Listening to business dialogues	• Reading business contracts	• Reading tables • Listening to meeting schedules
Activities	• Interviewing • Role-plays	• Information gap • Simulations	• Opinion gap • Group decision making
Grammar	• Relative pronouns to be used to describe people, places, companies • Coordinating conjunctions: *and, so, or, but*	• Modal auxiliaries to be used to express opinions on buying and selling products • Subordinating conjunctions: *after, when, since, unless*	• Wh-questions to be used at business meetings • Conjunctive adverbs: *additionally, consequently, however, likewise*
Vocabulary	• employer • employee • executive • manager • administrator	• sales • purchase • proposal • supplier • customer	• appointment • postpone • schedule • portfolio • presentation

Based on <A>, choose the TWO components in <B> that do NOT correspond to the teachers' ideas about their syllabus. Then explain your answers with evidence from <A> and <B>.

First Draft

_____

_____

_____

_____

_____

_____

_____

Revised Version

_____

_____

_____

_____

_____

_____

_____

03 **Read the passage in <A> and the email in <B>, and follow the directions.**
[4 points] 2023 전공B 6번

| A |

Ms. Hong, a new English teacher, had a hard time getting her students to talk in her English speaking class. She investigated the issue and found a checklist related to the problems that hinder the students' active engagement in speaking. The checklist consisted of seven categories with descriptions: no preparation time, uneven participation, poor listening ability, lack of speaking strategy use, mother-tongue use, nothing to say, and inhibition. Based on her observations, she evaluated how often her students struggled with the problems in the checklist during her English speaking class.

Class Observation Checklist

Descriptions	Scale		
	1	2	3
1. Students need some quiet time before they are engaged in a speaking activity.		✓	
2. In group activities, some of the students free-ride without contributing to the discussion.		✓	
3. Students have listening difficulties when engaged in speaking activities.	✓		
4. Students are not aware of speaking strategies and need to develop their own.			✓
5. When students speak the same mother tongue, they tend to use it in group work, especially when the teacher is far away.			✓
6. Students complain that they cannot think of anything to say.		✓	
7. Students are often inhibited from trying to say things in English in the speaking class.			✓

1=seldom, 2=sometimes, 3=often

02

Ms. Hong gave careful thought to six, out of the seven problems, that she checked as "sometimes" or "often" in the checklist. She came up with satisfactory solutions to four of the problems; but for the other two, she decided to ask for help. She sent an email about the two problems to Mr. Park, a head teacher, in order to seek some advice. He replied as in <B>.

B

From ∨	parkminsu5827@school.korea
To	∘ Ms. Hong (Teacher)
Subject	Re: Asking for advice

Dear Ms. Hong,

I am sorry to reply to your email so late. I have thought about the two problems you mentioned in your email, and my suggestions for the problems are, in brief, as follows:

The first problem arises quite often in speaking classes. If the task you want to do in class is based on group work, I think you need to choose a task such as jigsaw that we talked about the other day. When I included that activity in my English speaking class, the students' participation increased significantly overall while they were pooling all their information in groups.

The second problem is another one that happens frequently in English speaking classes. Why don't you appoint one of the group members as monitor? I think the very awareness that someone is monitoring helps the students put more effort into using the target language.

I hope these suggestions work well in your class. If you have any more questions or problems, please feel free to talk to me.

Best regards,

Park, Min-su

Based on <A> and <B>, identify the TWO problems Ms. Hong asked for Mr. Park's advice about. Then, explain why he made the suggestions for her two problems, respectively. Do NOT copy more than FOUR consecutive words from <A> and <B>.

First Draft

_____

_____

_____

_____

_____

_____

_____

_____

Revised Version

_____

_____

_____

_____

_____

_____

_____

_____

04 Examine the survey results in \<A\> and part of the interview with the teacher who taught Practical English Ⅱ in \<B\>, and follow the directions. [4 points] 2016 전공B 1번

A

A school administrator conducted a survey with 60 students from two classes of Ms. Lee's Practical English Ⅱ in order to improve the course in the future.

Evaluation of Practical English Ⅱ

Content	Number of respondents per category			
	1	2	3	4
(1) I feel I achieved my learning objectives as a result of taking this course.	4	9	25	22
(2) I feel more confident in my self-expression in English as a result of taking this course.	5	9	24	22
(3) I feel the supplementary material used in this course was helpful.	5	6	25	24
(4) I feel my speaking performance was assessed effectively based on the tests and assignments given.	29	22	8	1

1=strongly disagree, 2=disagree, 3=agree, 4=strongly agree

B

A: Your Practical English Ⅱ was very satisfying for students. What do you think made it so successful?

T: Well, I thought it was necessary to make decisions about what would be taught and how it would be taught before designing a course, so I did a survey and interviews.

A: You mean you chose the teaching materials, contents, and activities based on what your students wanted to learn?

T: That's right. The results also provided me with a lot of information about what my students needed to learn or change, their learning styles, interests, proficiency levels, etc. Based on that information, I decided on the course objectives, contents, and activities.

A : You must have been very busy working on designing the course before it started. What about assessment?

T : Students just took one major test at the end of the semester. I regret that I evaluated only their learning product.

A : You mean just once over the semester?

T : Yes, I thought it was impossible to assess their speaking performance regularly by myself and I gave one major test to the students. So I was actually unable to gather information on the developmental process of their speaking abilities.

. . .

A : Okay. Thank you for your time.

A=administrator, T=teacher

Describe ONE strong point with evidence of what the teacher did for the success of the Practical English II course. Then describe ONE weak point of what the teacher did in the course, and suggest ONE possible solution from the teacher's standpoint.

First Draft

_____

_____

_____

_____

_____

Revised Version

_____

_____

_____

_____

_____

05 Read the passages in <A> and <B>, and follow the directions. [4 points]

A

Ms. Min, a novice middle school English teacher, conducted a survey on the teaching practices of English teachers. She asked 47 local English teachers to vote for one principle they use most often for designing communicative activities. Her purpose was to find out design principles other teachers favored and then apply them to her own teaching. She analyzed the survey responses, and the results are shown below.

No.	Design Principles	Vote Counts
1	Utilize consensus-building activities in which students work together to come to an agreement on given topics.	3
2	Make activities personalized where students talk about their own thoughts, opinions, feelings, and experiences.	16
3	Allow students to choose from a list of topics to talk about so that activities are communicative and manageable.	8
4	Use tasks that require students to produce concrete and tangible outcomes, such as an itinerary or map, as a result of communication.	13
5	Employ fun and playful activities, such as games, that have a competitive element.	7
	Total Counts	47

B

After the survey, Ms. Min developed communicative activities by applying some of the principles.

[Activity 1]

Work in groups. Think about your life at the age of ten. Answer the questions below. Then talk to your group members and find out if you have any similar experiences.

☐ Do you remember your teacher? What was s/he like?
☐ Were there any places you particularly liked or disliked? Why?
☐ Who were your friends? What were they like?
☐ What did you use to do before/after school or during the breaks?
☐ What was your favorite game?

[Activity 2]

Work in pairs. Each student receives a different card. Ask questions to each other in turn about the things on your card.

Card A	**Card B**
Ask your partner questions about Australia: - about big cities and their locations - about native people	Ask your partner questions about Australia: - about its flag - about wildlife
Here are the answers to your partner's questions: - Flag:  - Wildlife: kangaroos, koalas, emus, a lot of animals not found elsewhere	Here are the answers to your partner's questions: - Big cities and their locations:  - Native people: Aboriginals, arrived 65,000 years ago, many tribes, have lived in harmony with the land

[Activity 3]

Work in pairs. Each student receives either Worksheet A or Worksheet B. Talk with your partner to complete Daniel's class schedule using the example dialogue below.

Example – S1 : Which class does Daniel have on Mondays at 9:00?
　　　　　 S2 : He has English.

02

Worksheet A

Daniel's Class Schedule

Time	Monday	Tuesday	Wednesday	Thursday	Friday
9:00-9:50		Korean			
10:00-10:50	Math		Physics	Biology	English
11:00-11:50		English			Spanish
11:50-13:00			Break		
13:00-13:50	Sports		Music	Sports	

Worksheet B

Daniel's Class Schedule

Time	Monday	Tuesday	Wednesday	Thursday	Friday
9:00-9:50	English		Spanish	Korean	Arts
10:00-10:50		Physics			
11:00-11:50	Biology		History	Math	
11:50-13:00			Break		
13:00-13:50		Music			History

Based on <A>, for each of the two most popular design principles, identify the ONE activity in <B> that the principle has been applied to, respectively. Then explain your answers with evidence from <A> and <B>.

First Draft

_____

_____

_____

_____

_____

_____

_____

_____

Revised Version

_____

_____

_____

_____

_____

_____

_____

_____

06 Read the passage in <A> and the teaching procedure in <B>, and follow the directions. [4 points] 2025 전공A 11번

A

　Ms. Kim, an English teacher, is selecting lesson objectives to implement into a new lesson. The following are the lesson objectives for reception and production.

Lesson Objectives

Reception
　R1. Students can recognize reduced sounds of words.
　R2. Students can identify specific details from a text or discourse.
　R3. Students can distinguish between literal and implied meanings.

Production
　P1. Students can explain the sequence of an event in the right order.
　P2. Students can write a simple journal, letter, or email.
　P3. Students can argue for and against a topic in a respectful manner.

B

Step	Teaching Procedure
Step 1	In groups, students brainstorm the pros and cons of using AI in education and create a mind map. convenient — distracting immediate feedback — Pros — AI — Cons — cheating no constraints — less human interaction place　time

Step 2	Students listen to an audio clip on AI and digital tools in class and complete a worksheet. ▶ Listen to the conversation carefully and follow the directions below. A. Mark the sentences True or False. 1. Sora says that the use of AI should be prohibited in the classroom. [True/False] 2. Inho asks an AI chatbot to do his assignment. [True/False] 3. Minji compares the outputs on a topic from three different AI chatbots. [True/False] B. Match the person with his or her concern. Inho • • Excessive screen time Minji • • False information Sora • • Theft of personal data
Step 3	Students work together and write rules for the use of digital tools in class. Class Rules for the Use of Digital Tools 1. *e.g., Never download software to a school device without permission.* 2. _____ 3. _____ ◆ Useful expressions for polite agreement or disagreement - I agree. That's a good idea. That's right. - I don't think/believe so. I don't agree/disagree (with you). - What do you think? Would you agree with me? Don't you agree?

Identify ONE lesson objective for reception and ONE lesson objective for production from <A> that the teaching procedure in <B> targets. Then, explain your answers, respectively, with evidence from <B>.

First Draft

_____

_____

_____

_____

_____

_____

_____

_____

Revised Version

_____

_____

_____

_____

_____

_____

_____

_____

07 Read the lesson procedure and write the TWO lesson objectives. Do NOT copy more than FIVE consecutive words from the passage. [5 points]

2015 전공A 서술형 1번

The following is a sample lesson plan of culture-integrated language learning for 2nd year middle school students.

Lesson Procedure

(1) Students watch a video clip that shows an experiment, which is summarized below.

> The experiment shows that American mothers used twice as many object labels as Japanese mothers ("piggie," "doggie") and Japanese mothers engaged in twice as many social routines of teaching politeness norms (empathy and greetings). An American mother's pattern might go like this: "That's a car. See the car? You like it? It's got nice wheels." A Japanese mother might say: "Here! It's a vroom vroom. I give it to you. Now give this to me. Yes! Thank you." American children are learning that the world is mostly a place with objects, Japanese children that the world is mostly about relationships. Relationships usually involve a verb. Verbs are more important in Asian languages than in English. Asians tend to use an expression like "Drink more?" rather than "More tea?" when they perceive there is a need. Americans are noun-oriented, pointing objects out to their children, naming them, and telling them about their attributes. Nouns denote categories.

(2) Students share their own experiences about noun-oriented expressions as opposed to verb-oriented ones, and discuss different ways of thinking for those expressions.

(3) Students do Activity 1 in order to learn a variety of noun-oriented English expressions.

<**Activity 1**> Fill in the blanks with appropriate words.

Verb-Oriented Expressions	Noun-Oriented Expressions
He works hard.	He is a hard worker.
My head aches.	I _____.
He is very humorous.	He has a good _____.
…	…

(4) Students discuss why noun-oriented expressions are more frequently used in English than verb-oriented ones.

(5) Students engage in the following activity to reinforce their awareness of the cultural difference between the West and the East.

> Q: If you have a bad cold, which of the following wouldn't you say?
> A: ① I've got a stuffy nose.
>   ② I have a runny nose.
>   ③ My nose is sick.

First Draft

_____

_____

_____

_____

Revised Version

_____

_____

_____

_____

08 Read the teacher log and follow the directions. [2 points] 2023 전공B 1번

Teacher Log

Skill-integration is considered more and more important in modern language learning, but I found that at any one time I was almost always teaching just one skill in isolation. As part of my development as a teacher, I wanted to integrate multiple language skills and pursue a more real-life style of communication. To do this, I first investigated my own class practices. I video-recorded eight lessons. After reviewing the video files, I found that in six lessons I taught only one skill. In the other two, I was only able to integrate listening and speaking but never reading or writing. I drew up a plan to integrate language skills more often. What I did was implement the project-based learning approach so that students could collaborate in groups to advance their projects. I conducted the experiments over the second half of the semester and gathered the data. Then, I video-recorded another eight lessons toward the end of the semester to test the effectiveness of the measure I had implemented. After I analyzed the videos and the data, the results were as follows: two of the lessons showed the integration of speaking and reading skills, two other lessons integrated reading and writing skills, and one lesson integrated all four skills! Based on these results, I feel the approach really improved my teaching practice and my ability to teach students with the four skills in an integrated fashion.

Fill in the blank with the TWO most appropriate words.

The log above describes how the teacher addresses a problem in the classroom and resolves it through a systematic process of inquiry. Sometimes referred to as teacher research or classroom research, _____ is considered an important part of self-reflective teacher development. It usually involves four steps: planning, acting, observing, and reflecting. Its major goal is to improve both student learning and teaching effectiveness.

Your Answer _____

Create a semantic map of classroom management based on your understanding.

Self
Mapping

Possible Answers

01   needs analysis

02   Skills and Vocabulary in 〈B〉 do not align with the teachers' syllabus. The syllabus focuses only on listening and reading as receptive skills, and does not include both receptive and productive skills. Additionally, it deals only with single words such as 'employer' and 'sales', except for multi-word units like collocations and idioms.

03   Ms. Hong asks for Mr. Park's advice about two problems: uneven participation and mother-tongue use. To address the first issue, he believes that using a jigsaw task can significantly increase students' overall participation. For the second, he suggests appointing a monitor, as the awareness of being observed motivates students to use the target language instead of their mother tongue.

04   One strong point is that the course was designed based on students' needs, which the teacher identified through a survey and interviews. A weak point is that speaking ability was assessed only once at the end of the semester, without tracking students' progress. As an alternative, the teacher could use portfolios to collect in-class performance samples and assess students' ongoing development over time.

05   Principle No. 2 is applied in Activity 1, which requires students to talk about their personal experiences about their life at the age of ten based on given questions. On the other hand, Principle No. 4 is utilized in Activity 3, which requires students to produce a concrete and tangible outcome, by completing 'Daniel's class schedule'.

06   One objective for reception is for students to identify specific details from an audio clip by marking statements as True or False and matching a person with their specific concern. Additionally, one objective for production is for students to argue for and against a topic in a respectful manner while discussing class rules for the use of digital tools, using useful expressions for polite agreement or disagreement.

07   The aim of the lesson is to help students explain the cultural and linguistic differences between Western and Eastern societies. It also encourages them to practice various noun-oriented and verb-oriented expressions.

08   action research

3 Textbook Evaluation and Adaptation, and Instruction Tools

>> Possible Answers p.105

01 Read the passage and follow the directions. [2 points] 2025 전공A 3번

Materials can be adapted by using different techniques such as *adding, deleting, modifying*, and *reordering*. For example, we can add materials when a language item is not covered sufficiently in the original materials. Materials that are too easy or difficult for learners can be deleted. Modifying can be used to make them more relevant to students' interests and backgrounds and to restructure classroom management. Reordering the sequence of activities is another technique, which includes separating items and regrouping them.

Consider the original material extracted from a grammar exercise book and its adapted version below. In the adapted version, the original exercise has been adapted by using the ① _____ technique.

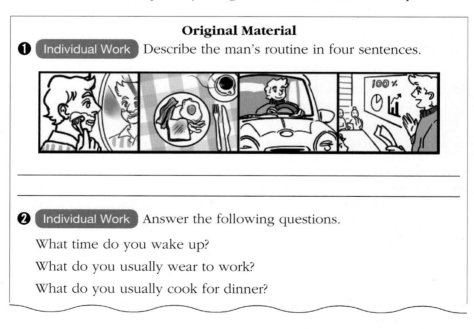

Original Material

❶ Individual Work Describe the man's routine in four sentences.

_____

_____

❷ Individual Work Answer the following questions.

What time do you wake up?

What do you usually wear to work?

What do you usually cook for dinner?

02

Adapted Material

❶ **Individual Work** Describe the student's routine in four sentences.

_____

_____

❷ **Pair Work** Work in pairs and ask each other the following questions.

What time do you wake up?

What do you usually wear on school days?

What do you usually eat for dinner?

Fill in the blank ① with the ONE most appropriate word from the passage.

Your Answer _____

02 **Read the conversation between two teachers and follow the directions.**
[2 points] 2020 전공B 2번

(Two teachers are evaluating two textbooks, Textbook A and Textbook B, in order to select the one that their students are going to use next year. This is part of their conversation.)

T1 : So, why don't we start with the first criterion? I went with Textbook A.

T2 : May I ask you why?

T1 : I think that the illustrations and graphics in Textbook A portray people in the target culture more realistically.

T2 : Yeah! Textbook A contains very realistic visuals that can provide our students with cultural information more accurately.

T1 : Good! Then, what about the second criterion?

T2 : Well, I think Textbook B is the better of the two. I couldn't give Textbook A a good score, because it appears to aim at explicit learning with many contrived examples of the language.

T1 : Hmm... could you clarify your point a bit more?

T2 : Well, I mean the texts and dialogues in Textbook A are oversimplified.

T1 : I had the same impression, but don't you think that they may help our students by focusing their attention on the target features?

T2 : You may be right, but I think that such texts might deprive them of the opportunities for acquisition provided by rich texts.

T1 : Oh, I see. That's a pretty good point.

T2 : So, in my opinion, Textbook B can provide more exposure to language as it is actually used in the real world outside the classroom.

T1 : Yeah! From that point of view, Textbook B will be intrinsically more interesting and motivating to our students.

T2 : I agree. Okay, then, I think we are ready to move on to the next evaluation criterion.

T=teacher

Fill in the blank with the ONE most appropriate word.

There are many criteria that can be used in textbook evaluation. The teachers, T1 and T2, are mainly focusing on, first, the criterion of reality of visuals and then, the other criterion of _____. In the dialogue, the latter is specifically related to language use shown in the textbooks.

02

Your Answer _____

03 Read the passages in <A> and <B>, and follow the directions. [4 points]

2024 전공 B형 7번

A

Mr. Kim, a middle school English teacher, attended a materials development workshop last week. There he learned that a variety of factors impact a learner's task performance which he could manipulate to adjust the level of task difficulty. One is language of input that learners have to process, such as the range and complexity of vocabulary and grammar. Another factor has to do with the processing demands of a task, which refer to the amount of mental effort required in working out answers. Besides these two factors, the conditions under which a task is performed also play an important role. Below are the notes he took during the workshop.

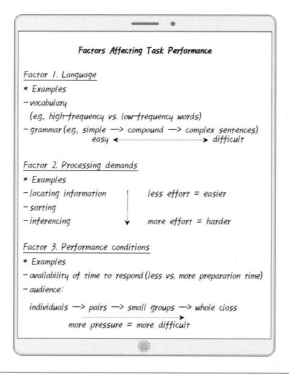

B

Based on what he learned at the workshop, Mr. Kim adapted one of the tasks from the textbook as shown below.

The original task

1. Read the following passage and answer the questions.

> Now we're going to see the most famous church in Britain, Westminster Abbey. Westminster Abbey is where the kings and queens have been crowned. We'll have about half an hour to look around the Abbey. We'll all meet again at the west door of the Abbey at four o'clock. If you get lost, then just call me. Remember it's a holy place, so behave yourselves.

   1) What is the name of the building that the people are going to see?
   2) Why are the people advised to behave themselves?

2. Choose a famous building or place in your neighborhood. Introduce it in front of the whole class.

The adapted task

1. Read the following passage and answer the questions.

> Now we're going to see the most famous church in Britain, Westminster Abbey. In Westminster Abbey, the kings and queens have been crowned. We'll have about half an hour to look around the Abbey. We'll all meet again at the west door of the Abbey at four o'clock. You may get lost. Then just call me. Remember it's a holy place, so behave yourselves.

   1) What is the name of the building that the people are going to see?
   2) Why are the people advised to behave themselves?

2. Choose a famous building or place in your neighborhood. Introduce it to your partner.

Identify the TWO factors in <A> that Mr. Kim addressed to adjust the difficulty of the original task in <B>. Then explain how each factor was addressed in the adapted task, respectively, with evidence from <A> and <B>.

First Draft

_____

_____

_____

_____

_____

_____

_____

Revised Version

_____

_____

_____

_____

_____

_____

_____

04 **Read Mr. Park's comments in <A> and examine the results of a textbook evaluation by a review committee in <B>. Then follow the directions.** [3 points]

2014 전공A 서술형 3번

A

Mr. Park : The goal of my class is to help students use the language to communicate and perform authentic tasks. So I want to spend most of my class time letting students rehearse tasks they need to perform outside the classroom. I also want my students to have a lot of opportunities to work together so that they can use their linguistic knowledge to convey meaning rather than just practice form.

B

Evaluation Criteria	Textbook A			Textbook B			Textbook C		
	1	2	3	1	2	3	1	2	3
pattern drill activities		✓		✓					✓
role-play based on real-life situations		✓				✓	✓		
pronunciation tips			✓	✓					✓
regular grammar review			✓	✓			✓		
group projects	✓					✓		✓	

1=poor, 2=average, 3=good

Considering the information in <A> and <B>, identify the textbook you would recommend for Mr. Park and provide TWO reasons for recommending it based on its characteristics.

First Draft

_____

_____

_____

_____

_____

_____

_____

_____

Revised Version

_____

_____

_____

_____

_____

_____

_____

_____

05 Read the passages and follow the directions. [4 points] 2017 전공B 2번

A

Materials can be adapted for many reasons, for example, to localize, to modernize, or to personalize. We can localize materials to make them more applicable to our local context. We can modernize materials when they are outdated in terms of English usage or content. We can also personalize materials by making them more relevant to learner needs and interests. Materials adaptation can be carried out by using a number of different techniques, as shown in the figure.

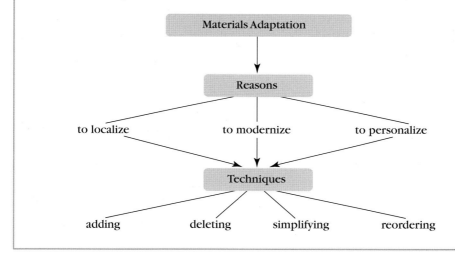

02

B

Mr. Lee is teaching first-year middle school students whose proficiency levels are very low. After conducting a needs analysis, he has learned that the students find the writing sections of the textbook difficult and that they are interested in sports. While he is planning a writing lesson for next week, he realizes that there is only one pre-writing activity in Unit 1 of the textbook. He thinks that one activity is not enough for his students to develop ideas for writing. Thus, he is going to increase the number of the pre-writing activities from one to three. In addition, thinking that the reading passage on sports in Unit 3 will better suit learner interests than the reading text in Unit 1, he decides to switch the two reading texts. He believes that this change will help his students become better prepared for writing and more engaged in English language learning.

Referring to the terms in <A>, explain the reason why Mr. Lee wants to adapt the materials, and identify which techniques he is going to use for materials adaptation. Do NOT copy more than FOUR consecutive words from the passage.

First Draft

_____

_____

_____

_____

_____

Revised Version

_____

_____

_____

_____

_____

06 Read the conversation and follow the directions. [2 points] 2021 전공A 1번

> T : Today, we are going to read a text about cooking. Are you interested in cooking?
>
> Ss : Yeah.
>
> T : Great. Let's study today's key words first. *(The teacher brings out kitchen utensils from a box.)* I brought some cooking utensils.
>
> S1 : Wow! Are those yours?
>
> T : Yes, they are. I use them when I cook. *(showing a saucepan)* You've seen this before, right?
>
> S2 : Yes. My mom uses that when she makes jam.
>
> T : Good. Do you know what it's called in English?
>
> S3 : It's a saucepan.
>
> T : Excellent, it's a saucepan. Everyone, repeat after me. Saucepan.
>
> Ss : Saucepan.
>
> T : And, *(showing a cutting board)* what's this in English?
>
> S4 : A board?
>
> T : Right, it's a cutting board. Good job. I also brought a couple of things from my refrigerator. This is one of my favorite vegetables. *(The teacher holds up an eggplant.)*
>
> S5 : Umm.... It's an egg...
>
> T : Nice try! It's an eggplant.
>
> T=teacher, S=student

Fill in the blank with the ONE most appropriate word.

> In this lesson, the teacher is using a type of supplementary materials called _____ to teach key vocabulary. Along with other visuals, these materials are expected to attract students' attention and to aid understanding and retention of vocabulary.

Your Answer _____

07 Read the passage in <A> and the table in <B>, and follow the directions.
[5 points] 2015 전공B 서술형 1번

A

　As part of an effort to maximize opportunities for her students to interact with others in English, Ms. Park, a high school English teacher, plans to design her lessons from a blended learning perspective. She is considering having the students interact with each other and her both online and offline. She designs lessons as follows: Online activities are based on a synchronous computer-mediated communication (CMC) interaction, and the transcripts of the online interaction are used a couple of days later for offline discussion.

　Realizing that many of her students seem shy, frustrated, and uncomfortable with face-to-face discussion, she would like to use a CMC tool to help students get ready for an offline discussion. By examining their online production with peers and the teacher, she believes that CMC activities will guarantee more equalized opportunities for participation and make students' errors more salient and thus open to feedback and correction.

B

Evaluation of Three CMC Tools

Criteria \ Tools	Tool A	Tool B	Tool C
Easy to Use	Y	Y	Y
Saving and Archiving	Y	N	Y
Real-Time Interaction	N	Y	Y
Video Chatting	N	Y	N
Online Dictionary	Y	N	N

Y=Yes, N=No

Based on the information in <A> and <B>, identify the tool you would recommend for Ms. Park, and provide TWO reasons for your recommendation.

First Draft

_____

_____

_____

_____

_____

_____

_____

Revised Version

_____

_____

_____

_____

_____

_____

02

Create a semantic map of textbook evaluation and adaptation, and instruction tools based on your understanding.

Possible Answers

01   modifying

02   authenticity

03   Mr. Kim adjusts the task difficulty based on Language and Performance conditions. He simplifies original compound sentences like 'where—' and 'if—clause' into easier grammatically simple sentences. For instance, 'In Westminster Abbey, the kings and queens have been crowned' and 'You may get lost. Then just call me'. He also asks students to present to their partners in pairs instead of in front of the whole class.

04   Since "role—play based on real—life situations" and "group projects" received high marks on the Evaluation Criteria, Textbook B could be recommended for Mr. Park. First, it enables students to use language for communication in real tasks, which aligns with Mr. Park's instructional goals. Second, group projects offer students many chances to work together and express their own meaning, unlike pattern drill activities that focus only on form.

05   Mr. Lee wants to personalize the textbook materials to better suit his students' needs for easier writing tasks and their interest in sports. To do this, he decides to add two pre—writing activities and reorder some reading texts to reflect learner interests.

06   realia

07   Tool C is the best choice for Ms. Park for two main reasons. First, it supports real—time interaction, which helps students get ready for offline discussion through synchronous communication. Second, it allows saving and archiving of students' online production, enabling the teacher to provide feedback and correction on students' errors.

Create a semantic map of the classroom contexts based on your understanding.

Self
Mapping

Build Up

Chapter
03

Practical Language
Teaching

Practical Language Teaching

1 Listening Skills

≫ Possible Answers p.116

01 Read the conversation in <A> and the lesson plans in <B>, and follow the directions. [4 points] 2025 전공B 7번

A

(Mr. Choi, a supervising teacher, is talking with his student teacher, Ms. Han, about her lesson plan.)

SupT : Ms. Han, I checked your lesson plan and found a couple of things that may help improve it.

ST : Oh, did I miss anything?

SupT : As you know, before you get to the main listening stage, we want students to recognize the purpose of listening, right?

ST : Yeah, and it sounds quite challenging. How can I do that?

SupT : You can try activating schemata. Making connections between personal experiences and learning can facilitate students' comprehension.

ST : Oh, I see.

SupT : And I recommend intensive listening. You know, authentic conversations have a lot of contractions. So, how about playing parts of a radio show focusing on particular language features?

ST : Good idea. Thank you. Is there anything else I missed?

SupT : Hmm, why don't you also try making some creative activities? Students can sing a song or chant, or they can record their own voice.

ST : Got it. I'll try to find some that are exciting.

SupT : Great. That's all I wanted to point out.

ST : Your suggestions are extremely helpful. I'll make some changes following your advice.

SupT : If you have any questions, don't hesitate to ask.

ST　 : I really appreciate your advice.

SupT=supervising teacher, ST=student teacher

B

After the conversation, Ms. Han revised her lesson plan based on Mr. Choi's suggestions. Below are the original and modified lesson plans.

Original Lesson Plan

Stage	Teaching & Learning Activities
Pre-listening	T shows the aim of the listening activity. T asks about what will happen to a person in a picture. T engages Ss in small talk.
While-listening	T asks Ss to listen to a story. T asks Ss to make inferences about the main topic of the story. T asks Ss to retell the story.
Post-listening	T asks Ss to write a summary on the story. T asks Ss to present on their summaries. T provides comments on Ss' presentations.

Modified Lesson Plan

Stage	Teaching & Learning Activities
Pre-listening	T presents the purpose of the listening activity. T asks Ss to predict what will happen to a person in a picture. T engages Ss in small talk.
While-listening	T asks Ss to listen to a story. T asks Ss to guess what the main topic of the story is. T asks Ss to do a gap-filling activity.
Post-listening	T asks Ss to summarize the story. T asks Ss to act out assigned scenes from the story. T provides feedback on Ss' performances.

T=teacher, Ss=students

Identify the supervising teacher's TWO suggestions from <A> that are reflected in the modified lesson plan in <B>. Then, explain your answers, respectively, with evidence from <B>.

First Draft

_____

_____

_____

_____

_____

_____

_____

Revised Version

_____

_____

_____

_____

_____

_____

_____

02 Read the passages in \<A\> and \<B\>, and follow the directions. [4 points]

2024 전공A 8번

A

Research suggests that L2 learners employ various listening strategies to increase comprehension of what they listen to. These strategies can be classified into two types: local or micro-strategies (Type 1) and global or macro-strategies (Type 2). Below are some specific strategies from each type.

Type 1
1) Identifying cognates
2) Using context to infer the meaning of words
3) Determining to skip unknown words or phrases

Type 2
1) Making predictions about the content based on titles or phrasal cues
2) Informing oneself about the context of the input (e.g., speakers, situations)
3) Recognizing the type of a listening text (e.g., news broadcasts, lectures, business presentations, job interviews)

B

In an attempt to improve his students' listening comprehension, Mr. Jung, a middle school English teacher, wanted to identify the strategies that his students apply to their listening process. In order to do so, he played a monologue to his students in class and paused the audio after each segment. He asked the students to think aloud while they were listening. Below are two of the audio segments Mr. Jung used and what Minji and Dongho, two of his students, were thinking as the audio was being played.

Audio Segment 1

I think social media is a waste of time. I'm totally addicted, I have to say. But there really isn't much going on.

Hmm, a waste of time? Maybe he's going to say something negative about using social media.

Minji

Audio Segment 2

I just spend hours just, sort of, checking other people's profiles, looking at their pictures. I don't know, it's a bit sneaky.

Sneaky? It's a new word. I don't think I need to know its meaning at the moment.

Dongho

Identify the ONE specific listening strategy from each type in <A> that Minji and Dongho applied to their listening process in <B>, respectively. Then explain your answers with evidence from <A> and <B>.

First Draft

_____

_____

_____

_____

_____

_____

Revised Version

_____

_____

_____

_____

_____

_____

Create a semantic map of listening skills based on your understanding.

Self
Mapping

Possible Answers

01   The supervising teacher provides two suggestions: intensive listening and creative activities. The student teacher incorporates these suggestions into the modified lesson plan. First, during the listening activity, the original story-retelling task is replaced with a gap-filling activity. Additionally, after listening, the student teacher plans for students to act out assigned scenes instead of merely presenting their summaries.

02   Minji and Dongho use different strategies for their listening process. Minji applies strategy (1) in Type 2, while Dongho uses strategy (3) in Type 1. Minji predicts negative aspects of social media based on the phrasal cue 'a waste of time', whereas Dongho skips the unknown word 'sneaky' in ⟨B⟩.

2 Oral Skills

≫ Possible Answers p.124

03

01 Read the passage in <A> and the teacher's log in <B>, and follow the directions. [4 points] 2021 전공A 8번

A

In an attempt to better understand language development, a three-tiered approach has been proposed, encompassing the following components for investigating production changes: complexity, accuracy, and fluency. Complexity generally refers to the lexical variety and syntactic elaborateness of the learner's linguistic system. Accuracy involves the correct use of the target language, while fluency concerns a focus on meaning, automatization, and real-time processing. These three constructs can be applied to appraise written or spoken language skill (i.e., performance) as well as to assess the state of the linguistic knowledge that supports this performance (i.e., proficiency).

B

Teacher's Log

In order to evaluate the progress of their speaking ability, I usually have my students read a story and then tell about it in their own words. It's not easy to measure all aspects of their speech at once. On the part of the students, it's also not easy to focus on more than one aspect simultaneously. So, I usually give my students two presentation opportunities and ask them to pay more attention to one aspect over the others in each presentation session. In the first presentation session, I focus on how naturally and clearly the content is delivered. To that end, I evaluate students' presentations based on the speed of their talk and the number of pauses and false starts. For the second presentation session, I record and transcribe the students' oral performance for a closer look. At this point, the presentation is evaluated especially by calculating the ratio of independent and dependent clauses and tallying the number of different verbs used.

Based on <A>, identify the component that the teacher focuses on in each presentation session mentioned in <B>, respectively. Then, support your answer with evidence from <B>. Do NOT copy more than FOUR consecutive words from <A> and <B>.

First Draft

_____

_____

_____

_____

_____

_____

_____

_____

Revised Version

_____

_____

_____

_____

_____

_____

_____

_____

02 Read the passage in <A> and the conversation between two teachers in <B>, and follow the directions. [2 points] 2020 전공A 3번

| A |

The way you speak is affected in many ways. For example, how much attention you are paying to your speech may be one factor. When you are not paying much attention to the way you are speaking, your speech may be more casual. By contrast, if you are conscious about the way you are speaking, your output will be less casual. The social position of the person with whom you are engaging in conversation may also affect your language output. It is natural to use more formal language when you speak to someone whose social position is above yours. The sociolinguistic concept of solidarity should also be considered. If your interlocutor comes from the same speech community or shares a similar social or cultural identity with you, you will feel connected to him or her, and this will affect the way you deliver your message. In addition, where you are affects the formality of your output. When you are in a formal situation, such as a business meeting, you naturally use more formal language, and the opposite is true as well. Lastly, the channel or medium of language, that is, whether you deliver your message through speech or writing, can be another critical factor that affects your speech. All of these things need to be considered carefully, because they constitute what is called pragmatic competence which relies very heavily on conventional, culturally appropriate, and socially acceptable ways of interacting.

B

T1: What are you writing?

T2: Oh, this is a recommendation letter for Miri.

T1: I see. She is very active in school activities, so you must have a lot to write about her.

T2: Yes, she is a good student, but she doesn't know how to adapt her conversational style when making a request.

T1: Hmm... what do you mean by that?

T2: When Miri approached me, she said, "Hi, teacher, can you write me a recommendation letter?"

T1: Haha... I understand what you mean. Some of my students also seem to have trouble making their speech style appropriate to the situation. Miri is just one example.

T2: Exactly! Still, I feel it's my responsibility to show them how speech styles differ across various situations. Hey, why don't we offer a special lecture on this topic?

T1: Definitely! We can invite a guest speaker who can show the importance of selecting the appropriate conversational style to match the _____ of the situation.

T=teacher

Fill in the blank in <B> with the ONE most appropriate word from <A>.

Your Answer _____

03 **Read the dialogue and follow the directions.** [2 points] 2019 전공A 3번

T: What are you going to do this weekend?
S: I will go to a market with my mom.
T: Is there anything you want to buy?
S: Eggs. Many eggs.
T: Is that all you want?
S: No. I will buy many bread and cheese, too.
T: (1) <u>Well, you said you will buy... buy...</u>
S: Buy bread and cheese. Ah, buy a lot of bread. I will buy a lot of bread and cheese.
T: Why will you buy them?
S: I like to make sandwiches. I will make many sandwiches.
T: Do you have any other plans?
S: I have many homework so I will study for many hours.
T: (2) <u>Well, what word do we use with homework?</u>
S: Many homeworks? No, a lot of? Yes, a lot of homework.

T=teacher, S=student

Fill in the blank with the ONE most appropriate word.

_____ refers to a type of the teacher's corrective feedback that directly induces the correct form of an error from the learner. One technique of this is to induce the correct form of an error by prompting the learner to reformulate the error and complete his or her own utterances, which is seen in the teacher's first corrective feedback, (1), in the dialogue. Another technique is to use questions to lead the learner to produce correct forms as shown in the teacher's second corrective feedback, (2), in the dialogue.

Your Answer _____

04 Read the passage and fill in each blank with TWO words. (Use the SAME answer for both blanks.) [2 points] 2017 전공A 7번

S : Could you give me some advice on how I can improve my pronunciation?

T : Yes, of course. Are you having trouble pronouncing a particular word?

S : I can't think of any right now, but there are a lot of sounds in English that I can't pronounce.

T : Can you give me an example?

S : The word *right*. *R* is very difficult for me.

T : Oh, that's because the consonant *r* doesn't exist in the Korean sound system. Then, you should practice pronunciation with a lot of _____. For example, the words *river* and *liver* have only one sound difference in the same position, but it makes a big difference in meaning.

S : Oh, I see. So, I guess *fine* and *pine* would be another example of _____, right?

T : Yes, you're right. If you want to be able to pronounce *right*, you first need to be able to hear the difference between *right* and *light*. There are so many other examples, like *rice* and *lice*, *rode* and *load*, etc.

S : I can't hear the difference between those words, either.

T : I know they are difficult, but with enough practice, you will be able to hear the difference and pronounce them correctly.

T=teacher, S=student

Your Answer _____

Create a semantic map of oral skills based on your understanding.

Possible Answers

01 The teacher focuses on fluency and complexity in each presentation session. In the first session, fluency is assessed by examining how smoothly students deliver their content, specifically looking at their speech rate, pauses, and false starts. In the second session, complexity is evaluated by analyzing the ratio of main and subordinate clauses and counting how many different verbs are used.

02 formality

03 Elicitation

04 minimal pairs

3 Reading Skills

>> Possible Answers p.137

01 Read the passages in <A> and <B>, and follow the directions. [4 points]

2025 전공A 12번

A

Metacognitive awareness of reading strategies is considered a conscious procedure utilized by readers to enhance text comprehension and encourage active reading.

Understanding its importance, Ms. Yu, a high school English teacher, used the Metacognitive Awareness of Reading Strategy Questionnaire to measure students' awareness on three categories of reading strategies. These include Global Reading Strategies (GLOB), Support Reading Strategies (SUP), and Problem-Solving Strategies (PROB). She also interviewed her students after the survey.

The Metacognitive Awareness of Reading Strategy Questionnaire

Category	Item	1	2	3	4	5
GLOB	G1. I have a purpose in mind when I read.					
	G2. I think about what I know to help me understand what I read.					
	G3. While reading, I decide what to read and what to ignore.					
	G4. I take an overall view of the text to see what it is about before reading it.					
	...			...		

SUP	S1. I paraphrase what I read to better understand it.					
	S2. I take notes while reading to help me understand what I read.					
	S3. While reading, I translate from English into my native language.					
	S4. I use reference materials (e.g., a dictionary) to help me understand what I read.					
	...				...	
PROB	P1. When the text is unclear, I re-read it to increase my understanding.					
	P2. I try to guess the meaning of unknown words or phrases.					
	P3. I adjust my reading speed according to what I am reading.					
	P4. I try to visualize information to help understand what I read.					
	...				...	

1=never, 2=occasionally, 3=sometimes, 4=usually, 5=always

B

Based on the survey results, Ms. Yu conducted interviews with the students who reported low ratings in the survey. Parts of the interview excerpts are below. One of the interview questions was "Do you feel challenged while reading?" After the interview, Ms. Yu identified reading strategies that students need to promote their active reading skills.

Interview Excerpts

S1: "I thought reading was just about understanding the words. When I don't understand something, I tend to skip over it. I think if I try to draw a picture in my mind when I'm not sure, I'll understand texts much better."

S2: "I usually analyze texts sentence-by-sentence until I fully understand them. After checking my low ratings on the questionnaire, I found that reading selectively may help me become a more efficient reader."

S=student

03

Identify the TWO items of reading strategies in <A> that Ms. Yu may apply to her reading instruction in relation to <B>. Then, explain your answers, respectively, with evidence from <B>.

First Draft

_____

_____

_____

_____

_____

Revised Version

_____

_____

_____

_____

_____

02 **Read the worksheet in <A> and the class observation note in <B>, and follow the directions.** [4 points] 2023 전공A 9번

A

Worksheet

Family History

Group Name:_____

Student Number & Name:_____

Role	Assignment	Student Assigned
Discussion Leader	Keeping the conversation going if it falters	
Passage Chooser	Choosing three passages that are important to the story to discuss	
Word Master	Showing the meanings of new words	
Grammar Checker	Using syntactic clues to interpret the meanings of sentences	
Story Summarizer	Summing up the story briefly	
Online Manager	Posting the activity outcome to the web or social network service	

• Before Reading

Can you guess who will mention the following statements? Match the pictures of the characters in the story with their corresponding statements.

• While Reading

Based on the text about the Brown and the Garcia families, complete the following figure.

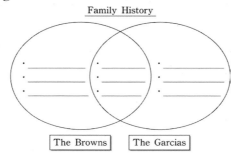

Family History

The Browns   The Garcias

• After Reading

What do you think about the characters in the story? Complete the sentences.

1. I feel sorry for _____ because _____.
2. I think _____ is a nice person, but _____.

B

Mr. Han's Class Observation Note

2. How did the teacher use teaching aids?	I set up a Reader's Club using a metaverse platform. While doing the reading activity in an online environment, each student took a specific role. I checked students' comprehension of the passage using the worksheet.
3. Did all the students participate actively?	The students looked absorbed in reading the three paragraphs of the text. After the reading activity, they actively participated in the discussion, carrying out their assigned roles. S1 managed the discussion and controlled each student's speaking time. S2 used an online dictionary when one student asked the meaning of a word, 'crane', and shared a picture of a crane with its meaning. S3 selected one linguistically complex sentence and explained its structure to the other students. S4 uploaded the summary that S5 wrote to the cloud and posted it on the class blog. Lastly, S6 selected another three paragraphs that they would read in the next class.
4. Did the students use suitable reading strategies?	During the discussion, students used various reading strategies such as activating schema, allocating attention, previewing, skimming, scanning, and criticizing. My students were pretty good at making guesses based on the pictures. I also noticed that using a graphic organizer helped students comprehend the story. By comparing and contrasting the two families, they extracted information from the text. My students understood the text very well based on the figure.

S=student

Identify the role that S2 performed in the group activity with the TWO most appropriate words from <A>, and identify the tool that Mr. Han used at the 'While Reading' stage in <A> with the TWO most appropriate words from <B>. Then, explain your answers, respectively, with evidence from <A> and <B>. Do NOT copy more than FOUR consecutive words from <A> and <B>.

First Draft

_____

_____

_____

_____

_____

_____

_____

Revised Version

_____

_____

_____

_____

_____

_____

_____

03 Read the conversation between two teachers and follow the directions.

[2 points] 2019 전공A 2번

> T1: My students are having trouble with plural nouns. I'm thinking of trying a new task.
>
> T2: What's your idea?
>
> T1: I'm planning to give a short text where every seventh word is blanked out. Students have to guess the correct word for each blank to make a complete sentence.
>
> T2: Well, that might be a bit difficult for beginning level students. I did a similar activity last semester. I gave a text where I blanked out only plural nouns so that students could focus on them.
>
> T1: Oh, I see.
>
> T2: You can also give students only parts of words in the blanks and ask them to restore each word in the text.
>
> T1: Hmm, that seems interesting. Well, then, for my students, I'll try to use only plural nouns in the written text and ask my students to fill in the blanks. Thanks for the suggestion.
>
> T1=teacher 1, T2=teacher 2

Complete the comments by filling in the blank with the ONE most appropriate word.

> In the above dialogue, the two teachers are talking about teaching plural nouns through three types of gap-filling tasks which require students to read the texts and fill in the blanks. The gap-filling described by the teachers here is _____, which can be readily adapted for pedagogical tasks in classrooms.

Your Answer _____

04 Below are an excerpt from a reading text and part of a student's think-aloud data generated while reading it. Based on the think-aloud data, identify the reading strategy that the student is using. Use ONE word. [2 points]

2014 전공A 기입형 10번

Computers have the potential to accomplish great things. With the right software, they could help make science tangible or teach neglected topics like art and music. They could help students form a concrete idea of society by displaying on screen a version of the city in which they live.

In practice, computers make our worst educational nightmares come true. While we bemoan the decline of literacy, computers discount words in favor of pictures or video. While we fret about the decreasing cogency of public debate, computers dismiss linear argument and promote fast, shallow romps across the information landscape. While we worry about basic skills, we allow into the classroom software that will do a student's arithmetic or correct his spelling.

> Well, nightmares? The author thinks computers do harm to education.

> Hmm . . . the author is blaming computer software for a decline in basic skills.

Your Answer _____

05 **Read the passage in <A> and the master plan in <B>, and follow the directions.** [4 points] 2022 전공 A 8번

A

   Ms. Yoon is an English teacher at a local middle school. According to her school curriculum, students should be able to use a combination of top-down and bottom-up processing when they practice the receptive skills of English, that is, listening and reading. Bottom-up processing is the processing of individual elements of the target language for the decoding of language input, while top-down processing refers to the use of background knowledge in understanding the meaning of a message. Now, she is developing a master plan for one of the units she will teach next semester. To help her students achieve this curriculum goal, she makes efforts to ensure that both bottom-up and top-down processing are practiced during each lesson period.

B

Ms. Yoon's Unit 1 Master Plan

1. **Lesson**: Challenge & Courage

2. **Objectives**
   Students will be able to:
   • listen to a dialogue and explain the content
   • ask for reasons and make decisions
   • read a text and retell the story

3. **Study points**
   • Functions: asking for and giving reasons
   • Forms: passive, subject-verb agreement

4. Time allotment : 8 periods, 45 minutes each

Period	Section	Learning Activities
1st	Listen 1	• Listen to a series of phrases for consonant/vowel linking between words • Listen to short sentences to discriminate between rising and falling intonation
2nd	Listen 2	• Listen to a dialogue and find the main idea • Do a sentence dictation activity with the active and passive voice
5th	Read 1	• Read the introductory paragraph and predict what will come next • Distinguish sentences containing subject-verb agreement errors
6th	Read 2	• Recognize whether a sentence is in the active or passive voice • Change base forms of verbs into the past participle by adding '-ed / -en'

Based on <A>, identify TWO periods in <B> in which the teacher focuses on both types of processing. Then, explain your answers with evidence from <B>.

First Draft

_____

_____

_____

_____

Revised Version

_____

_____

_____

_____

Create a semantic map of reading skills based on your understanding.

Possible Answers

01 Ms. Yu may instruct S2s to "decide what to read and what to ignore" from G3, encouraging them to avoid analyzing texts sentence-by-sentence and instead focus on reading selectively. Additionally, she can guide S1s to "visualize information" from P4, helping them picture what they read to enhance comprehension.

02 As a group role, S2 performs a word master, who presents the meaning of the new word 'crane' along with a related image. During the 'While Reading' stage, Mr. Han uses a graphic organizer that guides students to compare and contrast the two families and organize the extracted information in a visual format.

03 cloze

04 inferencing

05 In the 2nd and 5th periods, Ms. Yoon incorporates both top-down and bottom-up processing. In the 2nd period, students identify the main idea of a dialogue after listening, which involves top-down processing, and then complete a sentence dictation activity focusing on active and passive voice, reflecting bottom-up processing. In the 5th period, predicting what comes next requires top-down use of background knowledge, while identifying subject-verb agreement errors involves bottom-up analysis of grammatical forms.

03

4 Writing Skills

>> Possible Answers p.151

01 Read the passage in <A> and part of a lesson procedure in <B>, and follow the directions. [4 points] 2019 전공A 14번

A

(Below are suggestions from a conference for teaching L2 writing.)

To help students to write effectively...

(a) Start with pre-writing activities with little emphasis on ungrammaticalities and incorrect spelling.
(b) Have drafting and revising stages in a recursive way.
(c) Provide meaning-focused feedback.
(d) Offer students opportunities to think about their own writing.

B

(The following is part of Ms. Song's lesson procedure for teaching how to write an argumentative essay.)

Steps

1. T provides background information about artificial intelligence and Ss watch videos related to the topic.
2. Ss discuss the topic in groups and brainstorm.
3. Ss sketch their ideas and write the first drafts, focusing on content.
4. T reviews Ss' drafts and provides corrective feedback that reformulates ill-formed expressions.
5. Ss revise their drafts once, based on the feedback, and then hand in their final drafts to T.
6. T asks Ss to write reflective journals about their writing.

T=teacher, Ss=students

Identify TWO suggestions from <A> that Ms. Song does NOT implement in <B>. Then, support your answers with evidence from <B>.

First Draft

_____
_____
_____
_____
_____
_____
_____

Revised Version

_____
_____
_____
_____
_____
_____

02 Read part of a lesson plan and follow the directions. [4 points] 2016 전공B 3번

Lesson Procedure

| Stage 1 | • T shows video clips on environmental campaigns.
• T encourages Ss to brainstorm.
• T asks Ss to discuss their previous experiences in pairs. | <Purposes>
✓To arouse Ss' interests and motivation
✓To activate Ss' _____ |

Stage 2

• T shows new words and structures, and then explains how to use them within a sentence.

New Words	Grammatical Structures
transportation, recycle, mayor,	to leave ~, leaving ~, to protect ~, protecting ~,

• Please circle the right form in the sentences.

> 1. We require you (to leave/leaving) your cars.
> 2. . . .

• T has Ss read an article related to environmental problems with the following questions in mind:

> • What are the problems?
> • What are the causes of the problems?
> • How can you solve the problems?

• T asks Ss to write down key words related to the topic.

<Trash Problems in Our City>

Problems	dirty roads, _____, _____
Causes	no trash cans, _____, _____
Solutions	recycling bins, _____, _____

Stage 2	• T instructs Ss to combine the key words into a phrase or a sentence. • T demonstrate how to connect sentences by using the markers in the box and asks Ss to write their sentences coherently. **Markers**: Now, Firstly, Secondly, So, Thus, As a result, Therefore, . . .
Stage 3	• T has SS write a suggestion letter to their mayor based on what SS wrote. *Dear Mayor,* _____ _____ • T distributes rubrics for peer-evaluation to Ss. • T asks Ss to exchange their drafts.

T=teacher, S=student

Fill in the blank in the <Purposes> box in Stage 1 with ONE word. Then identify ONE way the teacher directly prepares students to write a well-organized suggestion letter in Stage 2, and explain it with evidence. Do NOT copy more than FIVE consecutive words from the passage.

First Draft
_____
_____
_____

Revised Version
_____
_____
_____

03 **Read the passage in <A> and the conversation in <B>, and follow the directions.** [4 points] 2022 전공B 7번

A

One of the reasons we can communicate successfully, especially in writing, is because we have some understanding of genre, socially recognized ways of using language for particular purposes. Genre represents the norms of different kinds of writing shared among people within a particular community. The emphasis on the social dimension of genre is a major characteristic of genre-based approaches to teaching writing.

A genre-based writing instruction involves students in an in-depth analysis of texts in the genre in which they are going to be writing. In particular, students are asked to analyze three essential features of the genre using example texts: 1) the *context*, which includes the situation and audience, 2) the *content*, which indicates the information and message conveyed, and 3) the *construction*, that is, how the texts of the genre are typically constructed in terms of the layout and language. When students are done with this task, they are in a position to create their own writing within the genre.

B

Activity 1

(After conducting a reading lesson about volunteering, a middle school English teacher prepares a poster-making activity for recruiting volunteers. He plans to have his students analyze the features of the poster genre before they make their own posters.)

• Ask the students to share their volunteering experiences.
• Have the students examine the poster and answer the questions in the worksheet.

Worksheet

CALLING FOR
VOLUNTEERS
TO HELP WITH
COMMUNITY PROJECTS

Builders Painters Landscapers General Handy Men

SATURDAY, DECEMBER 18, 2021

Register at WENEEDYOU.COM or call us at 123-4567

1. Why are some words capitalized?
2. Does the poster use full sentences? If not, why?

Activity 2

(Believing writing reviews is an important skill that her students should be equipped with, a high school English teacher prepares a genre-analyzing kit with which the students figure out the characteristics of the book review genre.)

· Tell the students they are going to read a book review.
· Have the students use the genre-analyzing kit while reading the book review.

Book Review

"I Really Want the Cup Cake"
Written by Philip Kent
Illustrated by Terra Wang
Ages 3-5 | 20 Pages
Publisher: Green Books | ISBN: 978-1-338-95941-2
What to expect: Rhyme, Dessert, Self Control
(or lack thereof)

Honestly, who of us hasn't wanted to dive in, just a teeny, tiny bit, to that delicious-looking cup cake left on the table? Just a bite couldn't hurt, could it? In this hilarious story about a little boy and his dog, that's exactly what they are trying not to do.

Reviewers' Genre-Analyzing Kit

1. Who do you think the review is aimed at?
2. When would people write this kind of text?

Based on <A>, identify ONE essential feature of the target genre that each activity in <B> focuses on, respectively. Then, explain your answers with evidence from <B>.

First Draft

_____

_____

_____

_____

_____

_____

_____

_____

Revised Version

_____

_____

_____

_____

_____

_____

_____

_____

_____

04 **Read the conversation in <A> and the two writing drafts in <B>, and follow the directions.** [4 points] 2023 전공B 7번

| A |

(Mr. Min, a middle school English teacher, is talking with his student, Jinhee, about her writing.)

T: Jinhee, I think you put a lot of effort into this first draft.

S: Yeah. But I think I made many mistakes.

T: Don't worry. I'll give you some comments on the categories you need to improve so that you can revise your draft. Can you do that?

S: Yes.

T: Great. Let's begin with content. I like your story, but it'll be better if you add more details here. Do you remember that we discussed how to use supporting details last week?

S: Yes, I do.

T: Good. I also saw that you had problems with organization.

S: You're right. Many events are popping up in my mind, but I can't put them logically.

T: One way to solve the problem is to use linking words such as *and, so, but, however, then, thus,* and so on, in order to show a logical sequence of events.

S: I see.

T: Two more categories are vocabulary and grammar. These two expressions here need to be changed. Look up the appropriate expressions in a dictionary. In addition, swimed here and very not much here are not correct. Think about how you can correct them.

S: Okay.

T: If you have any questions, just let me know. I'm looking forward to reading your second draft.

S: Thank you.

T=teacher, S=student

B

<First draft>

I went to a game park with my family last weekend. When we arrived, we ate delicious snacks. I swimed in the pool. My father did not swim. My mother did it very not much. We went on the rides. It was very funny and smily. We were very tired. We took a taxi to come home.

<Second draft>

I went to a game park with my family last weekend. When we arrived, we ate delicious snacks. Both my brother and I love sweets. My brother got three cups of ice cream and I got strawberry cake. I swimed in the pool, but my father did not swim. My mother did it very not much. Then, we went on the rides. It was very funny and smily. We were very tired, so we took a taxi to come home.

Identify the TWO categories Jinhee revised in the second draft based on Mr. Min's comments in <A>. Then, explain how she revised the categories, respectively, with evidence from <B>.

First Draft _____

_____

_____

_____

Revised Version _____

_____

_____

_____

05 Read the passages in <A> and <B>, and follow the directions. [4 points]

2024 전공A 12번

| A |

Below are the posts made by two English teachers on an online teacher community where teachers can share their ideas and provide each other with help regarding the use of digital technology.

Teacher 1's Post

Posted by eng98

Any suggestion?

I'm teaching middle school students. My students are not interested in writing. I think it's because I'm the only one who reads their work. It seems they do not have a sense of an audience. If someone other than me reads their writing, I think they'll be more conscious of the quality of their work and put more effort into it. Also, if various multimodal resources are available, my students will be able to express their ideas more creatively. Can you recommend a technological tool that would be appropriate for my students?

💬 Comment ➹ Share

Teacher 2's Post

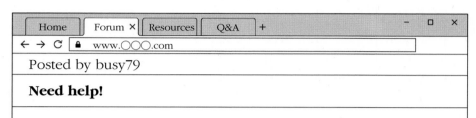

Posted by busy79

Need help!

I'm looking for a tool to help my students. They love to improve their interpersonal skills. But, as you know, it's extremely hard to provide enough opportunities for them to communicate with others. Even if I'm trying to incorporate as many speaking activities as possible in my lessons, it's still not enough. I think they need more opportunities to interact with others in English outside of the classroom. If the tool could help shy students feel less anxious without worrying about their self-image, it would be even better.

● Comment ➔ Share

B

Tool 1

This is a cloud-based quiz platform. Teachers can create quizzes to help learners to practice what they have learned. Various question formats are available including true or false, matching, multiple choice, etc. It generates a report of student performance after the quizzes are completed.

Tool 2

When teachers use this virtual reality simulation app, they can invite their students into the virtual space they have created. Students can communicate with others in English in simulated real-life situations taking place in airports, markets, and cinemas. Here students can create an avatar and converse with each other.

Tool 3

Students can use this voice recognition software in order to bridge the gap between oral and written language. They can read a text on screen and then record their voice. The tool also lets students know what errors they have made by highlighting them on the screen.

Tool 4

This is an online platform where students are encouraged to write and post their written work. The platform allows them to incorporate photos and graphics or embed videos into their work. Other students can then reply to the posts. The original writer can reply back as well.

Tool 5

Using this app, teachers can create a mind map for teaching English vocabulary. It shows groupings or relationships between words visually. Moreover, there is a link to an online dictionary. QR codes can also be created to share the mind map with students.

Based on <A>, for each teacher, respectively, suggest the ONE most appropriate tool in <B> that satisfies their needs. Then explain your answers with evidence from <B>. Do NOT copy more than FOUR consecutive words from the passages.

First Draft

_____

_____

_____

_____

Revised Version

_____

_____

_____

_____

Create a semantic map of writing skills based on your understanding.

Possible Answers

01   Ms. Song does not implement suggestion (b) and (c). Regarding (b), although the drafting and revising stages should be recursive, Ms. Song allows students to revise their drafts only once. As for (c), instead of providing meaning-focused feedback, she gives feedback that focuses on form by correcting ill-formed expressions.

02   Schemata
The teacher helps students write a well-organized letter by demonstrating how to connect sentences using transitional markers. After the demonstration, students construct coherent and well-paragraphed writing.

03   Activity 1 focuses on *construction*, and activity 2 focuses on *context*. In Activity 1, students examine the use of capitalized words and incomplete sentences to understand the layout and language typical of a poster. In Activity 2, students identify the audience and purpose of a book review by answering questions about for whom and when the review would be written.

04   Jinhee revises the second draft in terms of content and organization. First, she improves the content by adding more supporting details about who gets which snacks. Second, she enhances the organization by using a linking word, such as 'but', 'then', and 'so', to connect events logically.

05   Tool 4 is best for Teacher 1 as students upload their written works embedded with photos, or videos on an online platform, and then other students provide comments on the posts. Tool 2 is ideal for Teacher 2, as it allows students to converse with counterparts in English in simulated real situations using their avatars in a virtual space.

03

Create a semantic map of the receptive skills.

Self
Mapping

Create a semantic map of the productive skills.

5 Vocabulary & Grammar Teaching

>> Possible Answers p.170

01 Read the passage in <A> and the teacher's journal in <B>, and follow the directions. [2 points] 2020 전공A 1번

A

Vocabulary is a core component of language knowledge and provides much of the basis for how well learners listen, speak, read, and write. Without extensive knowledge of vocabulary or diverse strategies for acquiring new words, learners are often unable to produce as much language as they would like.

Knowing a word does not simply mean knowing its surface meaning. Rather, it involves knowing diverse aspects of lexical knowledge in depth including phonological and morphological forms and syntactic and semantic structures. Therefore, activities that integrate lexical knowledge of form, meaning, and use should be included in class.

B

Teacher's Journal

Ms. Kang and I read an article on teaching vocabulary and discussed how we can improve the way we teach vocabulary. We realized that we have been heavily focused on expanding the size of our students' vocabulary. As a result, they seem to know a lot of words but do not understand or use them properly in context. So, we came up with the following activities that we believe help our students develop _____ of vocabulary knowledge across form, meaning, and use.

Vocabulary activities to be implemented:
• Trying to pronounce the target words by listening to a recorded text
• Analyzing parts of the target words (e.g., prefixes and suffixes)
• Guessing the meanings of the target words using contextual cues
• Studying concordance examples to see various contexts and collocation patterns
• Writing a short story using the target words

Fill in the blank in <B> with the ONE most appropriate word from <A>.

(Your Answer) _____

02 **Read the passage in <A> and the word entries in <B>, and follow the directions.** [4 points] 2021 전공A 12번

| A |

A corpus is a collection of texts of written or spoken language from various sources presented in electronic form. It provides evidence of how language is used in real situations, from which lexicographers can analyze millions of examples of each word to see how real language behaves. Many contemporary dictionaries, therefore, incorporate the features derived from the analyses of corpus data, some of which are shown below.

1) Frequency : statistical data on how often words are used in the language

2) Collocation : information on what other words commonly occur with the word in focus

3) Context : information on which particular field (e.g., law, engineering, medicine) or social situation (e.g., formal vs. informal) a word is used in

4) Authentic example sentences : sentences from what users of the language actually write or say in books, newspapers, speeches, or recorded conversations, etc.

B

Both Dictionary X and Dictionary Y are developed in part by incorporating data from corpora.

Dictionary X

Shed [ʃed] **UK** ◀) **US** ◀)

verb *(past tense and past participle* **shed**,
present participle **shedding***)*
[transitive]

1. GET RID OF   to get rid of something that you no longer need or want
2. DROP/FALL   to drop something of allow it to fall

Word Partners

- *shed jobs/workers/staff*
- *shed weight/pounds/kilos*
- *shed an image*
- *shed your inhibition*
- *shed a load*
- *shed tears*

Dictionary Y

Shed UK ◀) **US** ◀) [ʃed]

verb [shedding], [shed], [shed]

1. [transitive] to get rid of something you do not need or want

USAGE BOX

Shed is mainly used in journalism. In everyday English, people usually say that one **gets rid of** something.

2. [transitive] to lose a covering, such as leaves, hair, or skin, because it falls off naturally, or to drop something in a natural way or by accident

With regard to the word 'shed,' identify ONE corpus-based feature described in <A> for each dictionary in <B>, respectively. Then, provide evidence from <B> for each feature that you choose.

First Draft

_____

_____

_____

_____

_____

_____

_____

_____

Revised Version

_____

_____

_____

_____

_____

_____

_____

_____

03 **Read the passages and the teaching journals, and follow the directions.**
[4 points] 2017 전공B 1번

A

Form-focused instruction (FFI) can be split into two types: focus on formS and focus on form. According to R. Ellis (2001), FFI "includes both traditional approaches to teaching forms based on structural syllabi and more communicative approaches, where attention to form arises out of activities that are primarily meaning-focused" (p.2).

B

Mr. Song

My students often tell me that they feel overwhelmed by the number of grammatical structures they have to learn. While thinking about ways to help students develop grammatical competence, I decided to teach grammar explicitly in class. Today I spent most of the class time on explaining grammatical rules using meta-linguistic terms. Although some of the students initially showed some interest in learning about the rules, many of them got bored, with some dozing off after ten minutes or so.

Miss Oh

Most of my students find grammatical rules difficult and boring. So I decided to implement a new approach. For this approach, I typed up the reading passage in the textbook and deliberately italicized the target structures, hoping that this would help my students notice how the target structures function. After I passed out the reconstructed reading passage, I had my students read it by themselves and then work together in groups, cross-checking their understanding.

Referring to the terms in <A>, identify the type of form-focused instruction exemplified in each of the teachers' teaching journals, and explain with supporting evidence from <B>. Do NOT copy more than FOUR consecutive words from the passage.

First Draft

_____
_____
_____
_____
_____
_____
_____

03

Revised Version

_____
_____
_____
_____
_____
_____
_____
_____

04 Read the passage in \<A\> and examine the teaching procedures in \<B\>, and follow the directions. [4 points] 2016 전공B 5번

A

Language learning can be classified into different types in various ways in terms of how learners process linguistic form to acquire rules that govern its use. One way is to distinguish inductive learning from deductive learning. This distinction is made by taking into account how a rule is learned in relation with its specific instances.

B

(Below are parts of two teachers' instruction procedures for teaching past tense verb forms in hypothetical conditionals.)

Teacher A's Class

- T explains to Ss that past tense verb forms should be used in sentences with *if* clauses to describe hypothetical situations.
- T asks Ss to complete sentences with appropriate verb forms to show hypothetical situations.

> 1. I _____ (can) fly to you, if I _____ (be) a superhero.
> 2. If he _____ (have) a time machine, he _____ (will) go back in time.

- T asks Ss to read a short text with sentences describing hypothetical situations.

> If I had a spaceship, I would fly to Mars. I would also build my own house there and live forever, if there were both oxygen and water. Unfortunately, I don't have lots of money to buy a spaceship. . . .

• T asks Ss to write a paragraph starting with the given expression.

> If I lived on Mars,. . .
> _____
> _____
> _____

Teacher B's Class

• T gives back the written texts about hypothetical situations Ss produced in the previous class and provides their reformulated texts T has produced at the same time. Only incorrect verb forms in Ss' writings are changed in T's reformulation as in the examples below.

> <A student's original writing>
> _____
> If I have last year to live over again, I will exercise more and eat
> less junk food because I can be healthier. I will spend more time
> with my friends and have better grades, if I am more active and
> watch less TV. . . .

> <The teacher's reformulated text>
> _____
> *If I had last year to live over again, I would exercise more and eat*
> *less junk food because I could be healthier. I would spend more time*
> *with my friends and have better grades, if I were more active and*
> *watched less TV. . . .*

• T asks Ss to compare T's reformulated sample with their writings and to underline all the words in the sample that are different from those in their writings.

• T asks Ss to find what the underlined words have in common and in what way they differ from the ones used in their original writings in terms of language form.

• T asks Ss to work out the rule that applies to all their underlined words based on their findings in the previous step.

T=teacher, S=student

Identify the type of learning applied to each class in <B> based on <A>. Then explain how each class orients students toward its identified type of learning with supporting evidence.

First Draft

Revised Version

05 Read the teacher's beliefs in <A> and the part of the lesson plan in <B>, and follow the directions. [4 points] 2024 전공B 11번

A

I believe that lesson goals should be framed from the students' perspective, focusing on what they can achieve through the lesson. Furthermore, I usually ask my students to vocalize these goals together. I also place importance on teachers trying to motivate their students. So, I seek out some interesting video clips online that can keep my students engaged. Crucially, I prefer inductive activities and try to provide learning targets within context. Lastly, I believe it's essential to conclude the lesson by summarizing the main points, and especially at the final stage, I like to ask referential questions that are more related to the students' life.

B

Stages	Teaching & Learning Activities
Introduction	• T and Ss exchange greetings. • T presents today's lesson objective on screen and reads it together with Ss: "We will be able to describe the meanings of words that express feelings."
Development #1	• T plays a video clip that shows different cartoon characters with a variety of emotional expressions. • T checks Ss' understanding of the video clip. • T provides reading passages that include the following words. *like, excite, love, bore, dislike, bother, worry, fear, annoy, confuse, believe, suggest, demonstrate, infer* • T asks Ss to underline the words that they do not know and infer the meanings from the context. • T asks Ss to circle the words related to feelings or emotions. • T asks Ss to look up the meanings of the unknown verbs in the dictionary.

Development #2	• T presents the target rules: "In English, it is more typical, more frequent, so unmarked, for the person who experiences emotional feelings to appear in the subject position of the sentence." • T tells Ss about the meanings of the two sentences: *Sue likes the dogs.* vs. *The dogs pleas Sue.* • T distributes the following handout. In the following sentences, the arrows indicate who experiences the feelings described by the verbs 'bothers' and 'loves.' (1) Julia loves her sister. (unmarked, more typical) (2) Julia bothers her sister. (marked, less typical) Sentence (1) is more typical, so unmarked, because the subject, *Julia*, experiences the feeling of love. Sentence (2) is marked because the object, *her sister*, experiences the feeling of being bothered. Now, let's work on the following sentences and determine whether they are unmarked or marked: a. Julia worried her sister. (ⓐ) b. Julia feared her sister. (ⓑ)
Consolidation	• Using the PPT slides, T recaps the main points of the lesson. • T asks questions: "In the sentence 'Julia confuses her sister,' who is being confused?" "If we say 'Julia upset her father,' who was upset, Julia or her father?" • T bids farewell to Ss.

T=teacher, Ss=students

Fill in the blanks (ⓐ) and (ⓑ) with "unmarked" or "marked." Then choose the TWO stages in <B> that do NOT correspond to the teacher's beliefs in <A>, and explain your answers with evidence from <A> and <B>.

First Draft

_____

_____

_____

_____

_____

_____

_____

_____

_____

Revised Version

_____

_____

_____

_____

_____

_____

_____

_____

_____

06 **Read the passage in <A> and examine the teaching procedure in <B>. Then follow the directions.** [3 points] 2014 전공A 서술형 6번

A

Processing instruction, a type of focus-on-form instruction, is based on the assumption that when processing input, L2 learners have difficulty in attending to form and meaning at the same time due to working memory limitations. Not surprisingly, they tend to give priority to meaning and tend not to notice details of form. Processing instruction uses several principles to explain what learners attend to in the input and why. Below are some of these principles.

The Lexical Preference Principle: In (1), both *-es* and *boy* convey the same information, 'the third person singular'. Yet, learners prefer to focus on the lexical item, *boy*, to arrive at meaning, and often ignore the grammatical item, *-es*, while processing the sentence.

(1) The *boy* stud*ies* in the library, not at home.

The First Noun Principle: Learners tend to process the first noun or pronoun they encounter in a sentence as the agent of action. For example, they may misinterpret (2) as "Jack collected the data for the project."

(2) *Jack* let *Joe* collect the data for the project.

The Event Possibilities Principle: Event possibilities refer to the likelihood of one noun being the agent of action as opposed to another. Since it is more likely in the real world that a dog would bite a man than the other way around, learners would likely misinterpret (3) as "The dog bit the farmer."

(3) The dog was bitten by the farmer.

In processing instruction, teachers provide students with structured input activities, taking into consideration the principles above. In a structured input activity, students are forced to attend to form in order to comprehend a sentence.

B

Teaching Procedure

1. Explicit Explanation

Explain how a past tense sentence is constructed in English. Then inform students of why they tend not to notice the past tense marker *-ed* and thus misinterpret past tense sentences.

2. Structured Input Activity

Have students read six sentences and decide whether they describe an activity that was done in the past or usually happens in the present. Then, check the answers together.

Sentences	Present	Past
(1) They watched television at night.	☐	☐
(2) They watch television at night.	☐	☐
(3) I walk to school on Mondays.	☐	☐
(4) I walked to school on Mondays.	☐	☐
(5) We played soccer on weekends.	☐	☐
(6) We play soccer on weekends.	☐	☐

Identify the principle in <A> that the teaching procedure in <B> focuses on. Then explain how the structured input activity in <B> helps students correctly process the target form for meaning.

First Draft

_____

_____

_____

Revised Version

_____

_____

_____

Create a semantic map of the vocabulary instruction based on your understanding.

Self
Mapping

Create a semantic map of the grammar instruction based on your understanding.

Possible Answers

01   depth

02   Dictionary X demonstrates the collocation feature by listing frequent word partners of 'shed', such as 'jobs,' 'workers,' and 'tears.' On the other hand, Dictionary Y presents the context feature by stating in the usage box that 'shed' is mainly used in the field of journalism.

03   Mr. Song uses the focus-on-forms approach, while Miss Oh uses the focus-on-form approach. Mr. Song explicitly teaches grammar using metalinguistic terms and spends most of the class time on grammatical rules, which indicates a focus on forms. In contrast, Miss Oh helps students notice the target structures by embedding them in the reading task, which aligns with a focus on form.

04   Teacher A's class demonstrates deductive learning because the teacher explicitly explains the rule of *if* clauses and then provides students with exercises to apply that rule. On the other hand, Teacher B's class promotes inductive learning by encouraging students to observe the teacher's reformulated texts and analyze the changes in verb forms, leading them to infer the rule on their own.

05   ⓐ marked ⓑ unmarked
Development #2 and Consolidation do not align with the teacher's beliefs in ⟨A⟩. Development #2 presents the target rule 'unmarked/marked' as deductive example sentences without context, instead of inductive activities that the teacher prefers. Additionally, Consolidation provides display questions rather than referential questions that are related to students' lives. For example, "In the sentence 'Julia confuses her sister," who is being confused?'"

06   The structured input activity in ⟨B⟩ is based on the Lexical Preference Principle in ⟨A⟩. In the activity, students encounter sentence pairs that share the same lexical meaning but differ in tense. This design prompts them to shift their focus from content words to grammatical forms. By distinguishing present from past through the −*ed* marker, students are guided to process form for meaning, thereby overcoming their tendency to rely solely on lexical items.

Memo

NEW
Build Up

Chapter
04

Classroom Assessment

Classroom Assessment

1 Assessment Principles

≫ Possible Answers p.186

01 **Read the conversation and follow the directions.** [2 points] 2024 전공A 1번

> T1 : Ms. Park, I hear that the provincial office of education is going to implement an Internet-based interactive English speaking test next year. What do you think?
>
> T2 : I think they're going in the right direction.
>
> T1 : But, you know, I'm not sure if we have enough human and material resources at the moment.
>
> T2 : Right. In order to develop such a large-scale test, we need to have test writers, raters, and item banks.
>
> T1 : Well, how would the office of education prepare for this in the short time available?
>
> T2 : The good news is that they're going to roll out pilot testing next month, starting with a small number of voluntary schools.
>
> T1 : Oh, I see. But I'm still wondering how they'll secure the resources necessary for full implementation.
>
> T2 : It seems they're going to recruit staff and technicians for the test centers while completing several preliminaries.
>
> T1 : Good. I guess in the mean time they can train teachers to write test items in order to construct the item banks.
>
> T2 : Right. I also heard the office of education has already laid out solid plans for that.

T1 : That's good to know. Then we'll be able to measure students' English speaking ability more effectively from next year.

T2 : For sure. It's a step forward for all of us working in English education.

T=teacher

Fill in the blank with the ONE most appropriate word.

In the above conversation, the two teachers talk about feasibility in the process of developing a large-scale test. The issues they discuss are related to one of the principles of language assessment or test usefulness, which is technically called _____.

04

Your Answer _____

02 **Read the passage and follow the directions.** [2 points] 2014 전공A 기입형 7번

At a high school English writing contest, contestants were given the instructions in the box and completed their compositions.

Listen to a taped radio interview of Barbara Carrel, a famous writer, about her adventure to Africa. While listening, take notes. Then using the notes, write a story about her adventure. You will be given 30 minutes to complete the story.

Each contestant's composition was evaluated by two English teachers using the same rating scale. Below is part of the two teachers' scoring results.

Ratings of Contestants' Compositions

Students	Criteria	Teacher A	Teacher B
Giho Lim	Content	2	5
	Organization	1	4
	Vocabulary	3	4
	Grammar	2	5
Bomi Cho	Content	3	1
	Organization	5	1
	Vocabulary	4	2

1=lowest ↔ 5=highest

Complete the comments on the situation above by filling in each blank with ONE word. Write your answers in the correct order.

The procedure used in the contest exemplifies (1) _____ testing in terms of the number of skills assessed. One potential problem with the scoring process is low (2) _____ reliability, which is most likely due to the subjectivity of the raters.

Your Answer   (1) _____

(2) _____

04

03 **Read the conversation and follow the directions.** [2 points] 2021 전공B 1번

(T1 is the head teacher, and T2 is teaching English writing this semester at the school.)

T1 : Good morning, Mr. Lee. How are your writing classes going?

T2 : Good morning, Ms. Park. They're going well, but I find scoring students' writing quite challenging.

T1 : What makes you say that?

T2 : I rated my students' writing assignments last night. But when I look at them today, I feel I would give different scores.

T1 : Why do you think that happened?

T2 : Well, I'm pretty sure it was because I was doing it late at night. I think I was too tired.

T1 : Mmm.... I don't grade my students' writing assignments when I'm tired. That way, I can avoid being inconsistent. I just put them away until the next day.

T2 : I bet that would be very helpful with keeping scoring reliable.

T1 : Yeah, it helps.

T2 : Another issue is that over time, I tend to stray from the rating criteria. I need to find a way to stick to it for consistency in scoring.

T1 : Well, why don't you go back every once in a while and check the last few essays you've marked to see that you're still following the rating criteria?

T2 : That's a good idea. It'll help keep me on track.

T1 : Exactly.

T2 : Thanks for your advice.

T=teacher

Fill in the blank with the ONE most appropriate word.

Teacher 1, the head teacher, is giving advice on the issue of _____ reliability that Teacher 2 is facing when scoring students' writing.

(Your Answer) _____

04 Read a teacher's and a student's journal entries and follow the directions.

[2 points] 2022 전공A 1번

> **Ms. Ahn's Journal**
>
> I think I need to change my approach to teaching speaking skills. In my conversation class, I usually have my students listen to dialogues and then practice the main expressions using pattern drills, which I thought would help them speak with both accuracy and fluency. However, when I assessed their speaking performance last week, most students had difficulties speaking fluently. They frequently had long pauses in their speech, but were quite accurate. In order to address this issue, I'm going to add more fluency activities such as discussion, role-plays, and information-gap activities.

> **Nayun's Journal**
>
> Today, I got my final exam results. Compared to the mid-term exam, my score has improved a lot. I'm very proud of myself because I studied a lot for the test. My English teacher usually includes lots of reading comprehension questions on exams, so this time I read all the reading texts in the textbook multiple times and took many practice tests. However, I'm a bit disappointed with the test in a way. I really want to improve my English writing skills, but I just don't have time to practice them. Well... I don't know.... I want to change how I'm studying, but I can't give up on getting good English test scores.

Fill in the blank with the ONE most appropriate word.

The above two journal entries demonstrate _____ effect in that the teacher and the student each write about what they do for their teaching and studying with regard to tests.

Your Answer _____

05 Read the passage and follow the directions. [4 points] 2020 전공B 6번

A high school teacher wanted to develop a test in order to assess his students' English reading ability. He developed the test based on the following procedures:

- Step 1: Construct Definition
  He started by clarifying what his test was intended to measure. He defined the construct of his English test as the ability to infer meanings from a given reading passage.

- Step 2: Designing Test Specifications
  According to the construct definition in Step 1, he specified the test as consisting of a total of 20 multiple-choice items: 1) 10 items asking test-takers to infer meanings and fill in the blank with the most appropriate words or phrases (i.e., Fill-in-the-Blank), and 2) 10 items for finding the best order of scrambled sentences (i.e., Unscrambling).

- Step 3: Developing Test Items & Piloting
  He finished item development. He piloted the test to examine whether the items had satisfactory test qualities.

- Step 4: Analyzing Item Facility & Item Discrimination
  He analyzed item difficulty. To increase internal consistency, he removed the items with a high value of item discrimination.

- Step 5: Analyzing Reliability & Validity
  Reliability was assessed by Cronbach's coefficient alpha. To investigate the concurrent validity of the test, he asked his colleagues to review the test items based on the test specifications.

- Step 6: Administering the Test
  After making the necessary revisions, he administered the test to his students.

Based on the passage above, identify TWO steps out of the six that have a problem in the process of test development. Then, support your answers with evidence from the passage. Do NOT copy more than FOUR consecutive words from the passage.

First Draft

_____
_____
_____
_____
_____
_____
_____
_____

Revised Version

_____
_____
_____
_____
_____
_____
_____
_____

06 Read the passage and follow the directions. [4 points] 2017 전공A 9번

Mr. Lee wants to determine how well the scores from the College Entrance Exam (CEE) predict academic success in college. The scatter plot below includes high school seniors' CEE scores from 2014 and their college Grade Point Averages (GPAs) in the fall of 2016. Their CEE scores are placed on the horizontal axis and their college GPAs on the vertical axis.

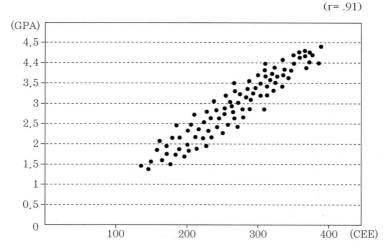

(r = .91)

r = correlation coefficient

Students	CEE (Fall 2014)	GPA (Fall 2016)
A	389	4.43
B	246	2.58
C	304	3.15
D	322	3.27
E	211	2.10
F	328	3.62
G	314	3.18
H	288	2.83
I	372	4.00
J	368	3.85
·	·	·
·	·	·
·	·	·

Based on the information in the passage, identify the type of validity within the context of criterion-related validation and explain it with evidence.

First Draft

_____

_____

_____

_____

_____

_____

_____

Revised Version

_____

_____

_____

_____

_____

_____

_____

Create a semantic map of assessment principles based on your understanding.

Possible Answers

01   practicality

02   (1) integrative (2) inter-rater

03   intra-rater

04   washback

05   Version 1

To increase internal consistency, in Step 4, the teacher should remove items not with high but with zero/negative item discrimination. In Step 5, as for the concurrent validity, he should ask his colleagues to check the correlation between the current test and previously validated test, not review the test referring to the test specifications.

Version 2

To increase internal consistency, in Step 4, the teacher should remove items not with high but with zero/negative item discrimination. In Step 5, as for the construct validity, he should ask his colleagues to review the given test referring to the test specifications.

06   The College Entrance Exam (CEE) demonstrates strong predictive validity, as its scores from 2014 show a high correlation with students' college GPAs in 2016. This means that the CEE scores effectively predict future academic success. For example, Student E, who received the lowest CEE score, had the lowest GPA, while Student A, with the highest CEE score, achieved the best GPA in college. This pattern supports the test's ability to forecast future performance.

2 Multiple-choice Item Testing

>> Possible Answers p.193

01 Read the passages in <A> and<B>, and follow the directions. [2 points]

2023 전공B 11번

| A |

A high school English teacher, Mr. Choi, wanted to learn how to write selected-response items (e.g., multiple-choice items) more efficiently. He wrote several items before the workshop began, and found some of them were flawed according to the guidelines he learned during the workshop. The following are some of the guidelines along with examples of flawed items.

> **General Guidelines for Writing Selected-response Items**
>
> ① Make certain that there is only one, clearly correct answer.
> ② State both the stem and the options as simply and directly as possible.
> ③ Present a single clearly formulated problem to avoid mixed content.
> ④ Avoid negative wording whenever possible. If it is absolutely necessary to use a negative stem, highlight the negative word.

Item 1

My forehead itches every day during the summer. Using sunscreen hasn't helped much. I think I'd better go to the _____ to get my skin checked.

　　　　a. dentist
　　　　b. optometrist
　　　　c. pediatrician
→　　　d. dermatologist

Item 2

Where did Henry go after the party last night?
　　　　a. Yes, he did.
　　　　b. Because he was tired.
→　　　c. To Kate's place for another party.
?　　　d. He went home around eleven o'clock.

Item 3

I never knew where _____.

      a. had the boys gone

→   b. the boys had gone

      c. the boys have gone

      d. have the boys gone

Item 4

According to the passage, which of the following is not true?

      a. My sister likes outdoor sports.

      b. My brother is busy with his plans.

→   c. My sister and I often do everything together.

      d. My brother is more energetic and outgoing than I.

'→' indicates the key; '?' indicates a possible answer.

B

    After the workshop, to improve the quality of the items, the teacher revised some items according to the guidelines. The following are the revised items.

Item 1

I think I'd better go to the _____ to get my skin checked.

      a. dentist

      b. optometrist

      c. pediatrician

→   d. dermatologist

Item 2

Where did Henry go after the party last night?

      a. Yes, he did.

      b. Because he was tired.

      c. It was about eleven o'clock.

→   d. To Kate's place for another party.

Item 3

I never knew _____.

      a. where had the boys gone

→   b. where the boys had gone

      c. the boys where had gone

      d. the boys had gone where

Item 4

According to the passage, which of the following is NOT true?

      a. My sister likes outdoor sports.

      b. My brother is busy with his plans.

→   c. My sister and I often do everything together.

      d. My brother is more energetic and outgoing than I.

04

Based on <A>, identify the ONE most appropriately revised item in <B> according to guideline ②, and the ONE most appropriately revised item according to guideline ③. Then, explain each of the items with evidence from <A> and <B>.

First Draft

Revised Version

02 Read the passages in <A> and <B>, and follow the directions. [4 points]

2024 전공B 6번

A

At a classroom assessment workshop, a teacher trainer taught how to interpret the results of an item analysis along with basic concepts of assessment using the data from an English reading test consisting of 25 multiple choice items. Table 1 shows the results.

Table 1. Results of Analysis

Item	IF	Item-Total Correlation	Alpha	Correlation with ERAT
1	0.48	0.57		
2	0.54	0.61		
3	0.39	-0.21	0.86	0.75
4	0.43	0.51		
5	0.33	0.55		

IF=Item Facility, ERAT=English Reading Achievement Test

The trainer explained the components of Table 1.

- Item difficulty (i.e., item facility) was measured by calculating the proportion of test takers who got the item correct.
- Item discrimination was assessed by item-total correlation which is a measure of correlation between an item and the total test score (a value of 0.3 or above indicating satisfactory discrimination).
- Internal consistency was measured by Cronbach's alpha (a value of 0.8 or above indicating satisfactory internal consistency).
- Evidence about the degree to which test scores agree with those provided by a test of similar construct administered at the same time was examined by correlation with the scores of the ERAT developed and validated by a well-known testing agency.

B

   The trainer asked six teachers to interpret the results. The following are their interpretations.

- Teacher 1: Of the five items, Item 2 shows the highest power of discrimination and Item 5 is the most difficult.
- Teacher 2: Item 3 should be carefully investigated in terms of the probability of miskeying and the construction of item response options.
- Teacher 3: There is a close relationship between the test takers' performance on Item 4 and the total test score.
- Teacher 4: The extent to which test takers' performances on this test are consistent is acceptable.
- Teacher 5: In order to increase the internal consistency of the test, Item 1 and Item 3 should be deleted.
- Teacher 6: The correlation between this test and the ERAT displays the evidence of predictive validity.

04

Identify the TWO teachers in <B> whose interpretation is NOT correct. Then support your answers with evidence from <A> and <B>.

First Draft

_____

_____

_____

_____

_____

Revised Version

_____

_____

_____

_____

_____

Create a semantic map of multiple-choice item testing based on your understanding.

Possible Answers

01 Item 1 in ⟨B⟩ is appropriately revised based on guideline ②, as the original long and complicated stem is rewritten into a single, clear, and direct sentence. Item 3 in ⟨B⟩ follows guideline ③, since it presents a single, clearly formulated problem. The revised version ensures consistency in tense among the options by changing them all to the past perfect form ("had gone"), avoiding confusion caused by mixed verb tenses in the original.

02 Teacher 5 and Teacher 6 misinterpret the item analysis results. Only Item 3 with a discrimination value of −0.21 should be removed to improve the internal consistency of the test, not Item 1 with a value of 0.57, above satisfactory value of 0.3. The correlation with ERAT indicates concurrent validity by measuring the degree of agreement between test scores and those provided by a similar test administered at the same time.

04

3 Performance-based Testing

>> Possible Answers p.204

01 **Read the dialogue and follow the directions.** [2 points] 2017 전공A 1번

Student—teacher Meeting

T : Well, looking back over the last twelve weeks, I can see that you have written many drafts for the three essay writing assignments.

S : Yes, I have. I have a lot of things here.

T : Of all your essays, which one do you think is the best?

S : I think the persuasive essay I wrote is the best.

T : What makes you think so? Maybe you can tell me how you wrote it.

S : Well... I think the topic I chose was quite engaging. I enjoyed the writing process throughout. And it feels good being able to see the progress I've made.

T : Yes, that's the benefit of this kind of project. I can see some improvement in your use of transitions. Your ideas are nicely connected and organized now.

S : Thanks. What else should I include?

T : Well, did you work on the self-assessment form and the editing checklist?

S : Yes, I did. I completed them and included them with all of my drafts right here.

T : Perfect! I'll be able to finish grading all of your work by the end of next week.

T=teacher, S=student

Complete the following by filling in both blanks with ONE word. (Use the SAME word.)

_____ can include essays, reports, journals, video or audio-recorded learner language data, students' self-assessment, teachers' written feedback, homework, conference forms, etc. As collections of these items, _____ can be useful for assessing student performance in that they can lead students to have ownership over their process of learning and allow teachers to pay attention to students' progress as well as achievement.

Your Answer _____

04

02 Read the passage in <A> and the part of the individual conference in <B>, and follow the directions. [4 points] 2020 전공B 10번

A

The students in Mr. Lee's class did an oral presentation. Mr. Lee gave his students the following rubric in advance and let them know that their performance would be evaluated across four categories: (a) content & preparation, (b) organization, (c) language, and (d) delivery. After the students' presentations were over, Mr. Lee had a conference session with each student to discuss his or her strengths and weaknesses.

PRESENTATION ASSESSMENT FORM

Evaluation Categories	Scale 1 poor 2 3 4 5 excellent				
I. Content & Preparation					
1. Interest & Value of topic	1	2	3	4	5
2. Informativeness of content	1	2	3	4	5
3. Preparedness	1	2	3	4	5
II. Organization					
1. Introduction (giving an overview)	1	2	3	4	5
2. Main body (supporting details & examples)	1	2	3	4	5
3. Conclusion (summarizing the presentation)	1	2	3	4	5
III. Language					
1. Accuracy (accurate use of grammar)	1	2	3	4	5
2. Appropriateness	1	2	3	4	5
3. Fluency	1	2	3	4	5
4. Pronunciation	1	2	3	4	5
IV. Delivery					
1. Confidence (not overly dependent on notes)	1	2	3	4	5
2. Gestures & Facial expressions	1	2	3	4	5

B

(The following is part of the individual conference that Mr. Lee had with one of his students, Yuna.)

Mr. Lee : Your presentation was pretty good.

Yuna : Thank you, Mr. Lee.

Mr. Lee : Yeah, you were really prepared. And so you got a perfect score on that area.

Yuna : I tried my best to make my PPT slides as informative as possible.

Mr. Lee : I know! They were really impressive. And your topic was really good.

Yuna : Thank you! How was my pronunciation?

Mr. Lee : Overall, I think your language was easy for the other students to follow. But you may want to try to use your language more appropriately. For example, some expressions you used like *you guys* and *you know*, may not be appropriate in this kind of presentation.

Yuna : I see. Thank you for your feedback.

Mr. Lee : I also noticed that you referred to your cue cards too frequently without looking at the audience.

Yuna : I did?

Mr. Lee : Yes, you did. Your presentation would have been much better if you had shown more confidence in your presentation task.

Yuna : I agree.

Mr. Lee : Other than that, everything looked fine.

04

Identify TWO of the four evaluation categories that Mr. Lee thinks reflect Yuna's weak points. Then, provide evidence for each identified category from <B>.

First Draft

_____
_____
_____
_____
_____
_____
_____
_____

Revised Version

_____
_____
_____
_____
_____
_____
_____
_____

03 **Read the passage in <A> and the tests in <B>, and follow the directions.**
[4 points] 2022 전공B 10번

| A |

Mr. Lee and Ms. Min are both middle school English teachers for 1st graders, but their students' English writing proficiency is quite different from each other. The two teachers have developed tests to assess their students' abilities to write using comparatives and superlatives as the target forms.

Mr. Lee's Assessment Note

• I taught my students to write simple sentences using comparatives and superlatives and provided sentence drill activities to practice them in previous lessons. After that, I designed a writing test to assess my students' abilities to make a simple sentence using one of the target forms.

Ms. Min's Assessment Note

• My students learned how to use comparatives and superlatives in sentences. After they were able to write sentences using the target forms accurately, I offered a story-writing activity in class. Then, I made a test to assess how well the students put sentences together to write a story using the target forms.

B

Test 1

Directions : Based on the pictures, fill in each blank with an appropriate comparative or superlative.

1. tall → _____

2. long → _____

3. big → _____

Test 2

Directions : Describe the two people circled in the picture by using one of the words listed below.

1. taller
2. younger
3. older

04

Test 3

Directions : Choose the correct answer.

My friends and I loved watching soccer on television, but we couldn't play it. We didn't have a team. Eventually, we made a soccer team and we were happy. Last Wednesday, we had a game, but it rained a lot. Our shoes got wet and heavy. The other team's players ran faster than us. So we took off our shoes.

Q. How was the weather last Wednesday?
    a. sunny   b. rainy   c. cloudy   d. snowy

Test 4

Directions : Describe the sequenced pictures using comparatives and/or superlatives. You should write more than THREE sentences with appropriate connectors.

Based on <A>, identify ONE test in <B> that each teacher developed, respectively. Then, explain your answers with evidence from <B>.

First Draft

_____

_____

_____

_____

_____

_____

_____

Revised Version

_____

_____

_____

_____

_____

_____

_____

Create a semantic map of the performance-based testing based on your understanding.

Possible Answers

01   Portfolios

02   Yuna shows weaknesses in terms of Language and Delivery. First, she uses informal expressions, such as 'you guys' and 'you know', which are not appropriate for a formal presentation. Second, she frequently looks at her cue cards instead of the audience, which indicates a lack of confidence in her delivery.

03   Mr. Lee developed Test 2, while Ms. Min developed Test 4. Test 2 asks students to write a simple comparative sentence to describe two people using one of the given target words. This matches Mr. Lee's focus on sentence-level practice using target forms. In Test 4, students are required to write more than three sentences using comparatives and/or superlatives with appropriate connectors. This matches Ms. Min's goal of assessing students' ability to use target forms in story writing.

Create a semantic map of all about the assessment based on your understanding.

Build Up

Chapter

05

기출지문분석

기출지문분석

1 2019학년도 기출지문분석

1 Topic : How to promote student learning (writing and speaking)

2 Focus

쓰기 활동과 말하기 활동 중에 교사의 재량으로 학습을 더 증진시킬 수 있는 방법을 제시하고, 이 방법들 중 수업에 적절히 반영된 것과 반영되지 않은 것을 고른 뒤 주어진 자료에서 각각의 증거를 찾아본다.

3 Classroom Data 2019 전공B 8번

A

Mr. Kim and Ms. Jo, English teachers, attended a workshop for language teachers where they both gained a lot of useful information to promote student learning. Below is part of the information from the workshop.

> **Teachers need to...**
> (1) keep in mind that their course goals and/or procedures can be modified.
> (2) offer students a variety of learning strategies to develop learner autonomy.
> (3) involve students in self-/peer-evaluation instead of evaluating them alone.
> (4) assess students frequently throughout the semester.

| B |

(Below are the two teachers' reflections after the workshop.)

Mr. Kim's reflection

To develop English writing abilities, my students engaged in writing activities. I simply assumed that paragraph writing would be enough for my students. However, I realized that I should change the initial course goal after assessing my students' first classroom writings. Their writing abilities were well above my expectations so I changed the goal set earlier and included essays. Since I believe that one-shot assessment at the end of the course is not effective for enhancing student learning, I carried out assessment periodically over the whole course period. I also believe assessment should be objective and that students' self-assessments are rather subjective in some ways. So, I did all the periodic assessments by myself, not asking students to evaluate their own work.

Ms. Jo's reflection

In my class, students were expected to develop debating skills in English. I organized my lesson in this way: brief mini-lectures, short video presentations to provide content for debating practice, followed by small group debating practice. I taught a range of learning strategies so that my students could become independent language learners utilizing those strategies whenever needed. For improving students' oral skills, I thought that arranging assessments multiple times, not just once, would be better. So I carried out assessments every two weeks during my instructional period. Based on the results of the assessments, I noticed that strictly following the lesson procedure was rather challenging to my students. However, I kept the same procedure over the course period since I believe maintaining consistency is crucial in order not to confuse students.

4 How to promote student's autonomy

(1) Begin new learning tasks with opportunities for students to ask questions and get help from their teacher or peers if they are having difficulty understanding the concepts.

(2) Provide students with meaningful choices consistent with learning objectives (e.g., what relevant topics they want to study) and exercises that encourage self-monitoring of their comprehension (e.g., becoming aware of their understanding of the materials) and tracking their learning progress (e.g., keeping track of their learning progress in a journal).

(3) Use specific praise that tells students what they did well and for which learning processes and skills they are being praised.

(4) Involve students in setting objectives and participating in decisions about how to individualize objectives in line with curriculum standards, plus individual and collective student interests and choices.

(5) In small group discussions, students can share their personal interests and then see how these fit with the teacher's list. By helping students define their personal learning goals and objectives, teachers can guide students to see whether these are consistent not only with their own interests but also how they can be aligned with curriculum standards and expectations.

(6) Appeal to student interest and curiosity by introducing the unfamiliar through the familiar.

(7) Reward success with praise and model how students can monitor their own progress and success with self-reward strategies.

5 Advantages of self-assessment

(1) Helps to develop important meta-cognitive skills.

(2) Increases self-awareness through reflective practice, making the criteria for self-evaluation explicit, and making performance improvement practices intrinsic to ongoing learning.

(3) Heightens their awareness of the goals and outcomes of the program and allows them to identify their strengths and needs in relation to those outcomes.

(4) Helps them identify how they learn best; reflect on what they can do as learners.

(5) Contributes to the development of critical reviewing skills, enabling the learner to more objectively evaluate their own performance—and others', when used in conjunction with peer assessment. With peer assessment they become more practised in giving constructive feedback, and receiving and acting on feedback received.

(6) Helps students to take control of their own learning and assessment, and giving them the chance to manage their own learning and development more independently.

(7) Gives students greater agency regarding assessment, thus enriching their learning.

(8) Possibly, in the long run, reduces the teacher's assessment workload—although on its own this benefit is not sufficient to introduce student self-assessment.

6 Keyword list

autonomy, agency, self-evaluation, peer-evaluation, formative test, summative test

2 2018학년도 기출지문분석

1 Topic : How to make a communicative classroom

2 Focus

Experienced teacher의 조언이 실제 수업에서 실현된 점과 실현되지 않은 점을 고르고 증거를 제시해 보도록 한다.

3 Classroom Data 2018 전공B 8번

A

(Below are notes that Ms. Shin, a new teacher, took of her senior teacher's advice on how to make her class communicatively oriented.)

Senior teacher's suggestions

- Objective : Get class centered on language functions rather than grammatical structures.
- Error targeted : Focus only on global errors impeding communication of meaning.
- Strategy : Encourage the use of communication strategies.
- Feedback : Provide correction implicitly.

| **B** |

(Below is Ms. Shin's talk at the beginning and closure of her single-activity class.)

Today, you are going to practice how to make requests using the question forms you learned from the last class. To do this, you will be doing an activity in pairs where you need to fill in a book order form by asking your partner for the necessary information. While doing this, you will get a chance to use the question forms to make requests. If you can't come up with the exact words to express the meaning you intend during the activity, you can try using similar words you know or even gestures, instead. Now, I will hand out the copies of the order form. Then, you can begin the activity with the student next to you. You'll work in pairs.
OK, here are your copies.

⋮

All right, now it's time to wrap up. I think you all did a great job on the form-filling activity exactly as I told you when the class started. But there is one and only one language element I want to briefly point out today. I noticed some of you missed 's' in some verbs like "He come" while talking. It should be "comes" not "come" though meaning is still clear without 's.' Apart from this, you seem to be fairly familiar with making requests now. Next time, we will focus on how to ask for permission.

4 Functional syllabus

A notional-functional syllabus is a kind of communicative syllabus which organizes units with the foundation of some functions such as asking question, expressing opinions, expressing wishes, making suggestions, complaining, and apologizing rather than including units instructing noun gender or present tense ending (Wilkins, 1976).

5 Communication strategies

Communication strategies are ways that learners get round the fact that they may not know how to say something. Most communication strategies are directed at filling in the gaps in the learner's vocabulary knowledge. If they help the speakers achieve their intended message, they are labeled achievement strategies. But the speaker might decide that the message is simply not achievable. Then they might adopt what is called an avoidance strategy.

6 Error correction

교사의 오류 수정의 정도는 어떤 오류를, 어느 정도로 수정하느냐가 관건이다. 오류 수정의 정도는 수업 목표에 따라 달라진다. 만약 정확성(accuracy)에 초점을 둔 수업이라면 global error뿐 아니라 local error도 correction의 대상이 된다. 이때 교사의 correction은 학습자의 발화가 끝난 후 실시하는 것이 바람직하다. 반면 유창성(fluency)과 의사소통(communication)에 초점을 둔 수업이라면 전체적인 의미에 영향을 주는 global error만을 대상으로 하여 학습자의 활동이 끝난 후 follow-up treatment에서 전체 교실 활동으로 실시해야 한다.

7 Keyword list

language functions, grammatical structures, global errors, local errors, error correction

Plus⁺

Coherence & Cohesion

The teacher provides a model text and students read it by focusing on coherence and cohesion of a model text.

▶ **Coherence** refers to the logical development of ideas within a text and it is an important subskill for students to be aware of.

▶ **Cohesion** refers to the grammatical and lexical connections between individual clauses. The grammatical links can be classified such as referents (pronouns, the article "the", demonstrative), ellipsis (leaving out of words or phrases where they are unnecessary), and conjunction (a word joins phrases or clauses together).

교사는 text의 coherence와 cohesion을 키워주기 위하여 다음과 같은 다양한 활동을 진행할 수 있다.

1. Focusing on the topic and function of each paragraph
2. Examining how the writer has chosen to order his arguments
3. Showing how to make their text "reader friendly"
4. Asking students to circle all the pronouns and then to use arrows to connect them to their referents
5. Asking students to replace a sentence which is missing from each paragraph or to replace the first sentence of each paragraph
6. Matching clauses which have been separated
7. Gapping conjunctions which students must replace from a selection

3 2017학년도 기출지문분석

1 Topic : How to manage a classroom

2 Focus

교사의 역할(teacher's roles)에 따른 수업 전개(classroom management)의 차이를 파악하도록 한다.

3 Classroom Data 2017 전공B 8번

A

Class A

Lesson objectives: Ss will be able to discuss and present their travel experiences using comparatives.

1. T tells a story about travel experiences.

> *Let me tell you about two trips I took, one to Singapore and the other to Bangkok. I really enjoyed my trip to Bangkok. It was more interesting than my trip to Singapore. Singapore was a little more boring than Bangkok. Although Singapore was cleaner and nicer; I thought Bangkok was a more fun city to travel in.*

2. T articulates the lesson objectives and asks Ss to form groups of six.

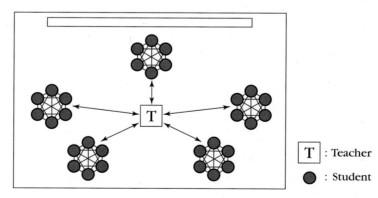

T : Teacher
● : Student

3. Ss begin a consensus building activity. During this activity, Ss compare locations according to a list of given adjectives (e.g., *safe, beautiful, historic*) on a worksheet.

(T helps Ss as needed.)

	Your chosen place	Your group's agreed-upon place
safe	*Busan*	*Daegu*
beautiful	*Jeju*	*Jeju*
historic		
...		
_____ (*your idea*)		

Ss compare and discuss their ideas using comparatives.
(T gives feedback. Ss correct ill-formed utterances.)

> S: Busan is beautifuler.
> T: Beautifuler?
> S: Beautiful, more beautiful.
> T: More beautiful?
> S: Busan is more beautiful.
> T: More beautiful. OK.

4. In groups, Ss discuss where the better and worse places to visit are.
   (T walks around the classroom to see if all the Ss are participating in the discussion. If Ss are reluctant to join in group work, T encourages them to participate.)

5. Ss work on a summary together within their group. T allows Ss to choose a role within their group (e.g., leader, timekeeper, note-taker, reporter).
   (T monitors their work and helps out as needed.)

6. Each group presents their summary to the class.
   ....

T=teacher, S=student

B

Class B

Lesson objectives :

(1) Ss will learn comparative forms;

(2) Ss will be able to make sentences using comparatives.

1. T explains the grammatical form of comparatives and writes the following chart on the board :

safe	safer
beautiful	more beautiful
cheap	cheaper
expensive	more expensive
...	...

(T stays at the front of the class the entire time, and Ss sit in orderly rows in silence.)

2. T instructs Ss to pay attention to the lesson.

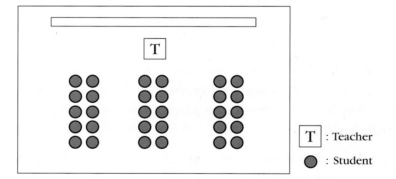

|T|: Teacher

● : Student

3. T plays a recording line-by-line, and Ss listen and repeat.

(T instructs them to repeat in unison.)

Recording	Students
A: What is cheaper, taking trains or taking buses? B: Taking buses is cheaper than taking trains.	What is cheaper, taking trains or taking buses? Taking buses is cheaper than taking trains.
A: Which one is safer? B: Taking trains is safer than taking buses.	Which one is safer? Taking trains is safer than taking buses.
....	....

4. T checks if Ss understand the comparative forms.

(T asks questions, Ss answer individually, and T gives feedback.)

> T: What is the comparative form of 'safe'?
> S: Safer.
> T: Good. What about 'beautiful'?
> S: More beautiful.
> T: Very good. Then what about 'cheap'?
> S: More cheaper.
> T: No, not 'more cheaper'. It's 'cheaper'.

5. Ss do more choral repetition.

(T plays the recording again, pausing it after key phrases, and Ss repeat them immediately.)

6. T asks Ss to repeat key phrases individually.

(T corrects Ss' errors explicitly.)

....

T=teacher, S=student

4 Teacher roles

(1) The controller

The teacher is in complete charge of the class, what students do, what they say and how they say it. The teacher assumes this role when a new language is being introduced and accurate reproduction and drilling techniques are needed.

In this classroom, the teacher is mostly the center of focus, the teacher may have the gift of instruction, and can inspire through their own knowledge and expertise, but, does this role really allow for enough student talk time? Is it really enjoyable for the learners? There is also a perception that this role could have a lack of variety in its activities.

(2) The prompter(facilitator)

The teacher encourages students to participate and makes suggestions about how students may proceed in an activity. The teacher should help students only when necessary.

When learners are literally 'lost for words', the prompter can encourage by discreetly nudging students. Students can sometimes lose the thread or become unsure how to proceed; the prompter in this regard can prompt but always in a supportive way.

(3) The resource person

The teacher is a kind of walking resource center ready to offer help if needed, or provide learners with whatever language they lack when performing communicative activities. The teacher must make her/himself available so that learners can consult her/him when (and only when) it is absolutely necessary.

As a resource the teacher can guide learners to use available resources such as the internet, for themselves, it certainly isn't necessary to spoon-feed learners, as this might have the downside of making learners reliant on the teacher.

(4) The assessor

The teacher assumes this role to see how well students are performing or how well they performed. Feedback and correction are organized and carried out.

There are a variety of ways we can grade learners, the role of an assessor gives teachers an opportunity to correct learners. However, if it is not communicated with sensitivity and support it could prove counter-productive to a student's self-esteem and confidence in learning the target language.

(5) The organizer

This is perhaps the most difficult and important role the teacher has to play. The success of many activities depends on good organization and on the students knowing exactly what they are to do next. Giving instructions is vital in this role as well as setting up activities.

The organizer can also serve as a demonstrator, this role also allows a teacher to get involved and engaged with learners. The teacher also serves to open and neatly close activities and also give content feedback.

(6) The participant

This role improves the atmosphere in the class when the teacher takes part in an activity. However, the teacher takes a risk of dominating the activity when performing it.

Here the teacher can enliven a class; if a teacher is able to stand back and not become the center of attention, it can be a great way to interact with learners without being too overpowering.

(7) The tutor

The teacher acts as a coach when students are involved in project work or self-study. The teacher provides advice and guidance and helps students clarify ideas and limit tasks.

This role can be a great way to pay individual attention to a student. It can also allow a teacher to tailor-make a course to fit specific student needs. However, it can also lead to a student becoming too dependent or even too comfortable with one teacher and one method or style of teaching.

Plus +

Plan and Flow

Too much free time can be a dangerous thing in a language classroom. An organized class that flows from one activity to another has a few benefits:
- Keeps students focused and in learning mode
- Maintains confidence in the teacher
- Prevents downtime, which leads to boredom and conversation

Don't stress about having a once-in-a-lifetime, cutting-edge curriculum planned for each class. What's more important is that students trust in your plan. They need to understand each activity, why they are doing it and what they will learn.

To help ensure a logical, efficient course plan that students trust, try scaffolding, backwards planning and balancing. To maintain class flow use scaffolding, in which you provide students with supplemental resources, instructions or activities that prepare or support them in order to make a given task more manageable. Here's a simplified summary of second language scaffolding for beginners.

For example, if you want students to read a news article and summarize it, you could :
- Have a class conversation on the topic beforehand to help familiarize them with it.
- Provide a vocabulary key with definitions and synonyms to refer to while reading.
- Have students work in pairs.

As students progress you will remove these "scaffolds" one by one. In a couple of weeks when students are more familiar with news articles, you could take away the vocabulary key and the pair work, keeping only the initial conversation. When you think they are ready, you will simply assign an article without any supplementary resources or activities.

Scaffolding helps you tailor activities so that they are neither too easy nor too difficult, keeping students from getting lost due to boredom or lack of motivation.

4 2016학년도 기출지문분석

1 **Topic**: Action research – Peer observation

2 **Focus**

Teacher training의 일환으로 교사가 자신의 수업 개선을 위해 수업 내용을 녹화하여 자가 장학(self-observation)을 하거나 경험 많은 동료 교사에게 장학을 부탁할 수 있다. 본 문항에서는 기존 수업의 활동 및 교사 질문에 대한 개선과 학습자의 오류에 대해 보다 적절한 피드백 등을 제안받고 있다.

3 **Classroom Data** 2016 전공B 8번

Teacher: Ms. Song	Consultant: Mr. Cho	Date: Dec. 2nd

Before consultation	In my class, I taught grammatical structures as follows: ･ ･ ･ T : She will go swimming. (showing a picture of 'John riding a bike') "Ride a bike." S1 : John will ride a bike. T : Good. (showing a picture of 'Mary playing the piano') "Play the piano." S2 : Mary will play the piano. T : Very good. (showing a picture of 'Tom visiting a museum') "Visit a museum." S3 : Tom visit a museum. T : No, you should say, "Tom will visit a museum." ･ ･ ･ T : (showing a picture of 'people going to a movie') What will they do? S4 : They will go to a movie. T : Very good. (turning to S5, showing a picture of 'students singing a song') What will they do? ･ ･ ･ I expected my students to learn practiced structures, but they still had difficulty in using them in real context.

Mr. Cho's advice	The following are pieces of Mr. Cho's advice: • Utilize an e-portfolio. • Use other types of questions. • Employ various authentic materials. • Provide other types of feedback. • Assign specific roles to students in group work.
After consultation	After the consultation, I made changes in teaching grammar as follows: T : Good morning, class. Winter vacation is coming soon. I will go to Jeju Island and travel around. Minji, what will you do this vacation? S1 : I go to Grandma's house in Busan. T : Minji, I go to Grandma's house? S1 : Oh... eh... I will go to Grandma's house. T : Perfect! What about Bora? Do you have any plans? S2 : Um... I... I take guitar lessons. T : I take guitar lessons? S2 : Uh... I will take guitar lessons. T : Good! What a great plan! Why do you want to do that? . . . .

T=teacher, S=student

4 Question types

(1) Display questions

They seek answers in which the information is already known by the teacher. This type of elicitation has been criticised for its lack of authenticity since it is not commonly used in conversation outside the classroom. Extensive use of display questions could be a waste of time. However, it is said that display questions can potentially be central resources which language teachers and students use to organize language lessons and produce language pedagogy. Accordingly, they are an important tool in the classroom, not only for the teacher to be able to check and test their learners, but also as a source of listening practice. One of the first things a beginner learns in English is how to understand and answer display questions.

Ex The teacher asks a learner 'What is the past simple form of leave?'

(2) Referential questions

They require answers which contain information unknown by the teacher, and they are frequently used to call for evaluation or judgement. They are commonly used in regular conversation outside the classroom, hence are believed to encourage students' higher-order thinking skills and authentic use of the second language in the classroom. Many teachers agree that teachers' use of referential questions could prompt students to provide significantly longer and syntactically more complex responses than the use of display questions.

Ex 1 What do you think about this topic?

What do you think about animal rights?

Ex 2 T : Last week we were reading "Kee Knock Stan" (title of a story). What is "Kee Knock Stan," (display Q) Hyunsoo?

S : I cannot understand.

T : Yes.

T : What do you think the postman at the post office would do? (referential Q)

S : I think I would divide it if the letters are to Hong Kong or other places.

T : Yes, I think that's a sensible way, right? Good.

05

5 2015학년도 기출지문분석

1 Topic : Reflection on today's lesson

2 Focus

Sumi와 Inho의 learning log와 교사의 teaching log에 있는 수업에 대한 comments를 통하여 수업의 장단점을 파악하고, 단점에 대해서는 적절하고 구체적인 해결책을 제공할 수 있어야 한다.

3 Classroom Data 2015 전공B 논술형 2번

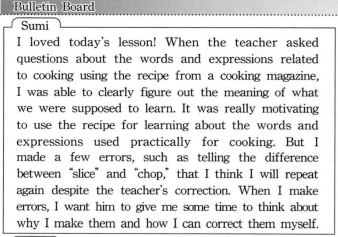

Bulletin Board

Sumi

I loved today's lesson! When the teacher asked questions about the words and expressions related to cooking using the recipe from a cooking magazine, I was able to clearly figure out the meaning of what we were supposed to learn. It was really motivating to use the recipe for learning about the words and expressions used practically for cooking. But I made a few errors, such as telling the difference between "slice" and "chop," that I think I will repeat again despite the teacher's correction. When I make errors, I want him to give me some time to think about why I make them and how I can correct them myself.

Inho

When the teacher asked us to bring a recipe from a cooking magazine yesterday for today's lesson, I wondered why. But when he asked questions about some words and expressions related to cooking using the recipes we brought, I realized why. When asking and answering about them using the cooking material with the teacher and then with my partner, I came to clearly understand the meaning of the words and expressions. Plus, it was very fun and exciting. But I didn't like that he corrected my errors when I misused the word "pan" in "boiling water in the pan"; I prefer getting correction from my friends because it makes me feel more comfortable.

My Teaching Log

What I put emphasis on in today's class

I always want my students to have a clear understanding of what I teach, so today I tried to teach the points using materials used in real life rather than the ones in the textbook. To my surprise, they really loved the way I taught today. They participated in the lesson with a lot of enthusiasm.

The things I have to improve in the next class

While leading the activity, for convenience' sake, I corrected the errors that students made. Considering their opinions, however, I have to use alternate ways to give them a chance to correct their errors individually or in pairs.

4 Error treatment

유창성을 넘어서 정확성에도 목적을 둔 교사는 학생이 생성한 오류를 수정할 것인지 아닌지에 대한 판단을 하고, 수정을 할 경우 언제, 어떤 방식으로 피드백을 제공할 것인지 결정하고 적절한 피드백을 선택하여 제공해야 한다.

- Should learners' errors be corrected?
- When should learners' errors be corrected?
- How should errors be corrected?
- Who should do the correcting?

교사는 학습자들의 참여를 유도하기 위해서 학생의 오류를 하나의 학습 과정으로 인식하고, 오류 수정은 학습 목표에 따라 진행해야 한다. 즉, 교실 수업의 목표가 정확성에 있는 경우 즉각적으로 피드백을 제공하지만, 의사소통에 초점을 둘 경우 의사소통 활동이 끝난 후에 피드백을 제공하는 것이 바람직하다.

When the focus is on meaning, it is inappropriate to interrupt the flow of interaction. In these situations, the teacher can make a note of errors for follow-up treatment later. When the focus is on form, the teacher might well interrupt before the students have finished their turn.

◈ Error Treatment Sequence (Lyster & Ranta, 1997)

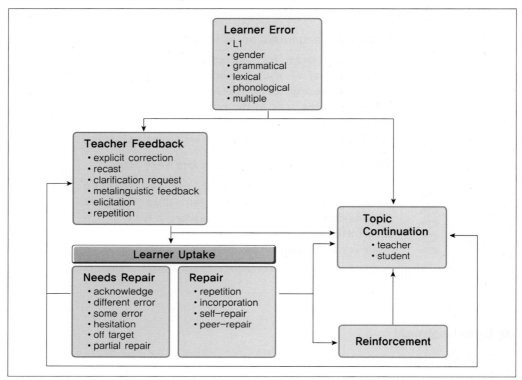

6 2014학년도 기출지문분석

1 Topic : Class observation

2 Focus

동료 교사의 수업 참관 후 작성된 observation checklist와 notes에 대한 분석을 기반
으로 수업의 특징에 대해 이해하고, 예상되는 문제점에 대하여 적절한 해결책을 제시할
수 있어야 한다.

3 Classroom Data 2014 전공B 논술형 2번

Observation Checklist

Instructor : Sumi Kim   Unit : 4. Personal Health

Topic : How to treat acne   Function : Giving advice

Period : 2/8   Date : Nov. 11

Areas	Criteria	Scale*
Lesson Preparation	• have a clearly developed lesson plan	1 —②— 3
	• prepare interesting multimedia materials	1 — 2 —③
Instructional Strategies	• give clear directions	1 —②— 3
	• use an appropriate grouping strategy for group activities	①— 2 — 3
	• provide level-appropriate activities	1 —②— 3
Affective Aspects	• create a warm and accepting atmosphere	1 — 2 —③

1=poor, 2=average, 3=good

Notes
- A fun video clip on acne. Ss loved it.
- T was kind and patient.
- Group activity (same-ability grouping)
  - Higher-level students did well. Had no problems.
  - Lower-level students had a hard time completing the task. Seemed like they needed some help.

---

4 Level-differentiated lesson

(1) Managing mixed level class

대집단 수업의 가장 큰 문제점 중 하나는 학생들의 언어능력에 차이가 난다는 것이다. 따라서 혼합된 능력을 지닌 학생들(mixed ability students)을 지도한다는 것은 교사에게 수업에 대한 계획 및 수행상의 여러 가지 문제점을 일으킨다.

Many teachers see mixed level classes as especially problematic. Yet in a real sense all classes have students with a mixture of different abilities and language levels. Within the school environments, students are often streamed—that is re-grouped for language lessons according to their abilities. In other situations, however, such placement and streaming are not possible and so teachers are faced with individuals who have different language knowledge, different intelligences, different learning speeds, and different learning styles and preferences. There is particular concern for the needs not only for students who are having difficulty at the lower end of the scale, but also for "gifted" students.

(2) Different student actions

학생들에게 상이한 자료 및 내용을 제공하기가 어려울 경우, 동일한 자료에 대한 상이한 반응 및 답변을 유도하는 것도 하나의 방법이 될 것이다.

① **Give students different tasks**: 동일한 읽기 자료를 제공하고 학생들에게 저마다 다른 답변을 하도록 요구한다.

For example, group A might have to interpret the information in the text by reproducing it in graphic form (or in charts and tables). Group B, on the other hand, might answer a series of open-ended questions. Group C—the group we perceive as having the greatest need of support—might be offered a series of multiple-choice questions; their task is to pick the correct response from two or more alternatives because we think this will be easier for them than having to interpret all the information themselves.

② **Give students different roles**: 과제 진행 시 학생들에게 저마다 다른 역할을 제시한다.

If students are doing a role-play, for example, in which a police officer is questioning a witness, we might give the student playing the police officer the questions they should ask, whereas the student playing the witness has to come up with their own way of expressing what they want to say. We will have done this because the student or students playing the police officer clearly need more guidance than the others. If students are preparing for a debate, we might give Group A a list of suggested arguments to prepare from whereas Group B (whom we think need less support) are told to come up with their own arguments.

5 Tiered tasks

수준별 그룹으로 진행하되, 과업 수행 결과물은 유사하다.

Example 1

다음은 '*The spirit of London*'이라는 읽기 자료를 토대로 구성된 3개의 과업 자료이다.

Top Tier

Task A: for weaker students

1. How much of London's history does *The spirit of London* show?
2. How do you go around it?
3. What special effects does it have?
4. What can you see in the modern-day section?

Answers

ⓐ light, sound, music, and smells
ⓑ police, punks, and tourist
ⓒ more than 400 years
ⓓ in a taxi

Middle Tier

Task B: for midlevel students

1. How much of London's history does *The spirit of London* show?
   ⓐ 400 years   ⓑ more than 400 years   ⓒ 300 years

2. How do you go around it?
   ⓐ in a taxi   ⓑ in a train   ⓒ on foot

3. What special effects does it have?
   ⓐ lights   ⓑ sound and music   ⓒ smells

4. What can you see in the modern-day section?
   ⓐ police   ⓑ punks   ⓒ tourists

Bottom Tier

Task C : for stronger students

1. How much of London's history does *The spirit of London* show?
2. How do you go around it?
3. What special effects does it have?
4. What can you see in the modern-day section?

- Matching work : Task A gives all the answers on the page for support. They are jumbled for challenge. Weaker students manipulate the given material, and can use logic to help match the task items, together with the information in the reading text.
- Multiple choice questions : Task B gives multiple-choice answers to help the average students. This is slightly different from the conventional "one answer only is correct" multiple choice, since in questions 3 and 4 there are more than one correct answer.
- Open questions : Task C gives open questions—with no extra support—to challenge the stronger students in the group.

Example 2

Tiered task의 보다 간단한 형태로 학생들의 수준을 두 단계로 나누어 동일한 과업을 진행하되, 교사가 과업의 support를 다르게 제공한다. Dual-choice gapfill이 이에 속한다.

The Dead Sad Animal Rap		MISSING WORDS
Listen to the rap. What are the missing words?		killed / shot easy / simple hunted / shot south / north
Humans...	ⓐ ... the dear old dodo,	
It was...	ⓑ ... It couldn' fly	
Humans...	ⓒ ... all the passenger pigeons	
From the...	ⓓ ... American sky.	

As they listen, weaker students circle one of the words in the box to fill each gap. Stronger students get the same task sheet, but with the missing words box cut off. The task is therefore more challenging for them.

7 2013학년도 기출지문분석

1 Topic : Dictogloss

2 Focus

Dictogloss 활동을 진행하는 각 단계 및 절차에 대한 이해를 토대로 각 단계 안에서의 문제점들을 파악하고, 학생들의 이해를 돕고 흥미를 이끌어내며 고른 참여를 이끌어낼 수 있는 실질적인 dictogloss 방법들을 제시할 수 있어야 한다.

3 Classroom Data 2013 논술형 1-2번

A novice high school teacher, Ms. Kim, uses dictogloss as a classroom task for the first time. She plans to use News Script to have students practice passive voice. The teacher's task description is below.

Task Description

- Inform students that the class will work on the dictogloss task with a specific focus on passive voice.
- Have students write down key words while they are watching the 7-minute-long news clip once.
- Ask students to work in groups of 8 for 20 minutes to reconstruct the story.
- Have students watch the clip one more time.
- Distribute the transcript and ask them to review it at home.

After the class, Ms. Kim wants to find out what students think about the dictogloss task. She asks the leader of each group to give comments. Their written comments are presented below.

1st group leader :

The story seemed interesting, but it went on and on. After watching it, we could barely remember anything we heard, except a few words like *boy, locked, shivering,* and *scared*. The teacher asked us to listen carefully for examples of passive voice, but we couldn't notice many. There were too many new and confusing expressions.

2nd group leader :

It was our first time to do this activity, so it was very, very difficult. Also, we didn't know anything about the story before watching the clip, so we were lost.

3rd group leader :

When we worked in groups, some students hardly had any chance to talk. So we could not share our ideas well.

4 Lesson procedure

✎ Required steps for a Dictogloss activity

Step	Students	Teacher
1. Preparation	• Study vocabulary activities to prepare for the text. • Discuss the topic (predict vocabulary and content etc.). • Move into groups.	
2. Listening for meaning	Listen to the whole text.	Reads the text at normal speed.
3. Listening and note-taking	Take notes listing key words.	Reads again at normal speed.
4. Text reconstruction in group	Work in groups to reconstruct an approximation of the text from notes (one learner acts as the writer).	• Helps groups. • Offers guidelines.
5. Text comparison between groups	Compare group versions of the text. Pay attention to points of usage that emerge from the discussion.	• Facilitates class comparison of versions from different groups. • Facilitates discussion and correction of errors.

* Steps 4 and 5 encourage learners to pay close attention to language form (i.e. word forms, word order, spelling, grammar rules, etc.)

8 2012학년도 기출지문분석

1 Topic A : How to develop a scoring rubric and rating scales

2 Focus

Scoring rubric 구성 시 가장 중요한 항목 중 하나인 구성타당도(construct validity)의 정의를 잘 이해하고 있고, 그것이 실제 시험(혹은 rubric)에서 문제가 되었을 경우에 어떠한 결과를 야기할 수 있는지에 대하여 예측할 수 있어야 한다. 더불어, 학생들의 실질적인 output에 대한 평가를 객관적으로 진행하여 scoring을 제공할 수 있어야 한다.

3 Classroom Data 2012 논술형 3-1번

A third-grade high school English teacher, Ms. Park, wanted to diagnose students' speaking ability and decided to use picture description as a performance assessment in her class. Ms. Park developed a scoring rubric and rating scales to evaluate students' performances. Then students were given a series of pictures and asked to describe them for three minutes as fully as possible. However, her head teacher, Ms. Yoon, commented on the initial scoring rubric and Ms. Park revised it. The following are pictures, transcripts of two students' picture descriptions, and Ms. Park's initial and revised scoring rubrics in tables.

<Pictures>

<Speech Transcripts>

<Jitae>

A family of three, uh, playing badminton.. erm.. on beautiful sunny day. It also look like, uh, they have set up, set up a tent and picnic in mountains. Wh.. Whi.. While they are away playing badminton, a eːr theːː dog, maybe a st.. st.. strayːː dog find their picnic and steal some food. The dog, dog runs away with a (0.8) sandwich in mouth. As soon as they come back to the camp siteːː, the family shocked to see the picnic, well, you know, ruined. He isːː hmm.. they obviously had, hmm, no idea what is going on. Then, after (1.2) packing up, I think, they head home? or motel, I mean, a place to stay. You can see people have, like, depressingːː erm depressed faces. To make thingsːː worse, it is getting dark. Th.. The.. Their car is still in the mountains.

<Mina>

I, er, I see happy family. hmm.. Father? Son? Some peopleːː people are playing (3.1) outside, at ground. Two eːr childrenːː playing with something like b.. ball. Big guy look at a boy and girlːː He is sitting on the chair. Oh, there is animal, one animal (2.4) a (2.0) dog or? (3.8) A big tent is open. It come in the mountain, oh fromːː the mountain? and run to the home. And dog try, tries to get some food and eːr eating that later. They are very (3.2) su.. sur.. surprised. Girl is angry. They? are angry. They have nothing to eat (2.9) no sandwiches or kimbab for the camping? He want to go home soon. It is dark eːr outside. (0.5) They take the.. the.. their car and areːː going back.

* Transcription Convention
(0.8) - Interval between utterances (in seconds)
eːr, theːː - Lengthening of the preceding sound

<Table 1> Ms. Park's <u>Initial</u> Scoring Rubric

	Jitae			Mina		
	Excellent	Good to Fair	Needs Work	Excellent	Good to Fair	Needs Work
Pronunciation	○			○		
Grammatical Accuracy		○			○	

<Table 2> Ms. Park's <u>Revised</u> Scoring Rubric

	Jitae			Mina		
	Excellent	Good to Fair	Needs Work	Excellent	Good to Fair	Needs Work
Pronunciation	○			○		
Grammatical Accuracy		○			○	
Fluency					○	
Cohesion	○					
Vocabulary	○				○	

Ms. Park's initial scoring rubric in <Table 1> has a big problem regarding the principle of validity. Also, if she used the test results from <Table 1> it would be problematic. In Ms. Park's revised scoring rubric two ratings are missing : ("Fluency" for Jitae and "Cohesion" for Mina).

4 Some examples of classroom testing

(1) Example 1

If you are trying to assess a person's ability to speak a second language in a conversational setting, asking the learner to answer paper-and-pencil multiple- choice questions requiring grammatical judgments does not achieve **content validity**.

(2) Example 2

I once administered a dictation test and a cloze test as a placement test for a group of learners of English as a second language. Some learners were upset because such tests, on the face of it, did not appear to them to test their true abilities in English. They felt that a multiple-choice grammar test would have been the appropriate format to use. A few claimed they didn't perform well on the cloze and dictation because they were not accustomed to these formats. As it turned out, the tests served as superior instruments for placement, but the students would not have thought so.

➡ 위와 같은 평가 상황은 안면타당도가 매우 낮으나(low face validity), 구성타당도가 매우 높다(high construct validity).

(3) Example 3 : Oral Interview

The scoring analysis for the interview includes several factors in the final score: pronunciation, fluency, grammatical accuracy, vocabulary use, and sociolinguistic appropriateness. The justification for these five factors lies in a theoretical construct that claims those factors to be major components of oral proficiency. So if you were asked to conduct an oral proficiency interview that evaluated only pronunciation and grammar, you could be justifiably suspicious about the construct validity of that test.

(4) Example 4 : Written Vocabulary Quiz

Likewise, let's suppose you have created a simple written vocabulary quiz, covering the content of a recent unit, that asks students to correctly define a set of words. Your chosen items may be a perfectly adequate sample of what was covered in the unit, but if the lexical objective of the unit was the communicative use of vocabulary, then the writing of definitions certainly fails to match a construct of communicative language use (Brown, 2004).

1 Topic B: Teaching and learning methods

2 Focus

제2언어 습득과 관련하여, 인지주의 접근법과 사회문화적 접근법에서 강조점을 두는 학습 원리들을 이해할 수 있어야 한다. 더불어, 그 두 가지 접근법을 기반으로 하여 Jitae의 학습 방법의 문제점을 인지하고 그 문제점을 극복하기 위한 적절한 활동들을 제시할 수 있어야 한다.

3 Classroom Data 2012 논술형 3-2번

| Context |

Ms. Park recognized Jitae's problem regarding the third-person singular subject-verb agreement after reviewing his speech sample from the performance assessment. Then Ms. Park had a conference with Jitae. She found that, in the first grade of middle school, Jitae was explicitly taught how to put -*s* at the end of verb stems and then practiced the subject-verb agreement through transformation exercises (e.g., *run → runs*). Since then, Jitae has been exposed to the grammatical morpheme through reading materials but has not been given chances to use the form in conversation. After checking up on Jitae's knowledge, Ms. Park was convinced that he still retained the grammatical knowledge about the rule. In the classroom, however, Ms. Park has observed Jitae making the same errors frequently in conversation.

4 CR tasks

학습자들에게 해당 규칙이 적용된 일련의 예들을 제공한 뒤 규칙을 도출하도록 하고 그 규칙을 자신의 상황에 맞게 적용, 연습하는 단계로 이루어진다.

Deductive means of teaching grammar tend to emphasize from over meaning, and promote passive rather than active participation of the learners in the learning process. Such approaches are believed to intimidate learners. Instead, awareness-raising inductive approach helps to develop learners' own understanding of language, and to build confidence in themselves as learners. Further, allowing the learners to take responsibility for discovering target rules favorably affects retention. Consciousness-raising tasks, which can be either deductive or inductive, offer an effective means of teaching grammar.

A CR task can be defined as a grammar activity where students are provided with L2 data in some form and required to perform some operation on or with it, the purpose of which is to arrive at an explicit understanding of some linguistic property or properties of the target language.

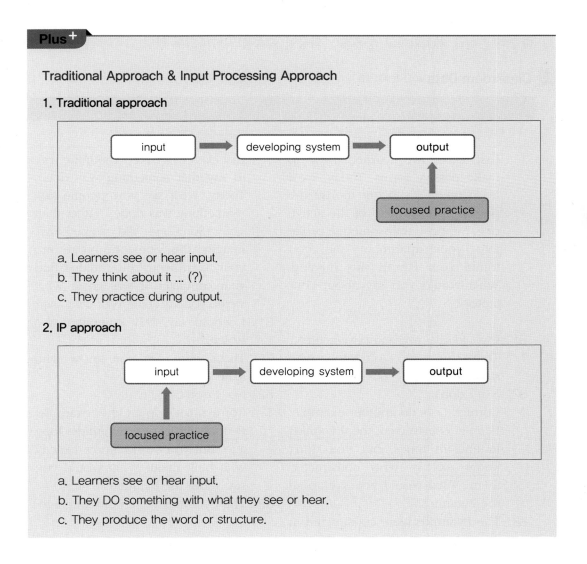

Plus⁺

Traditional Approach & Input Processing Approach

1. Traditional approach

a. Learners see or hear input.
b. They think about it … (?)
c. They practice during output.

2. IP approach

a. Learners see or hear input.
b. They DO something with what they see or hear.
c. They produce the word or structure.

9 2011학년도 기출지문분석

1 Topic : Level-differentiated lesson

2 Focus

Mixed levelled class 운영에 관련된 문항으로, 수준별 학습 과정을 토대로 teacher talk의 차이와 역할을 파악할 수 있어야 한다. 또한 과업에 대한 난이도 차이를 통한 학습의 손실을 최소화하고 성공적인 외국어 학습을 지향하도록 한다.

3 Classroom Data 2011 논술형 1번

Advanced Level	Intermediate-low Level
T : Last class, we learned how to make passive forms. Today, we'll learn when it's better to use the passive form instead of the active one. Suppose that someone broke into your apartment and you found your laptop was missing. What would you say about your laptop? S1 : I would say, "My laptop was stolen." T : That's right. Do you know who stole it? S2 : No, I don't. T : Correct. Let's do another example. People constructed the Pyramids in ancient times, but you don't know exactly who constructed them. What would you say about the Pyramids? S3 : The Pyramids were constructed in ancient times.	T : Last class, we talked about the way to say that something was done. Today, we'll see why people say, "Something was done," rather than say, "Someone did something." Imagine this. Someone broke into your apartment. You couldn't find your computer. It was gone! What would you say about your computer? S1 : I would say, "My computer was stolen." T : That's right. Do you know who stole it? S2 : No, I don't. T : Correct. Let's do another example. People built the Pyramids long ago. But you do not know exactly who built them. What would you say about the Pyramids? S3 : The Pyramids were built long ago.

T : Great. <u>Can anyone tell us when passive sentences are preferred to their corresponding active sentences?</u>

Ss: When we don't know who did something.

T : Good. Let's go through a passage together. Try to understand the passage, while also paying attention to the passive forms used in the passage.

TASK

Step 1

T : I'm going to read you the passage twice. First, I'll read it at normal speed and then I'll read it again as slowly as possible. As you listen, write down as many words and phrases as possible.

> Have you ever seen the Pyramids of Egypt? Have you ever wondered why they were built and how they were built? The Pyramids were built because the kings wanted to live after they died. They thought why they would live after they died. The Pyramids were constructed on the west side of Nile River. They were built there because the sun rises in the east and sets in the west. They believed why the king and the sun god would be born and born again, just like the sun. The Pyramids were very difficult to build, but the whole world can enjoy them.

T : Great. <u>So we can say the same idea two ways. We can say, "People built the Pyramids long ago." Or, "The Pyramids were built long ago." Now, when is it better to say, "The Pyramids were built long ago"?</u>

Ss: When we don't know who built them.

T : Good. Let's go through a passage together. Try to understand the passage. Let's see if you can find any sentences like "The Pyramids were built long ago."

TASK

Step 1

T : I am going to read you the passage twice. Both times, I will read it very slowly and clearly. As you listen, write down any words you hear.

> Have you ever seen the Pyramids of Egypt? Have you ever wondered why they were built and how they were built? The Pyramids were built because the kings wanted to live after they died. They thought why they would live after they died. The Pyramids were constructed on the west side of Nile River. They were built there because the sun rises in the east and sets in the west. They believed why the king and the sun god would be born and born again, just like the sun. The Pyramids were very difficult to build, but the whole world can enjoy them.

05

Step 2

T : Now, in groups of three, share your notes and see whether your group can come up with its own version of the text. Once your group has reconstructed the text, check it to make sure the meaning is similar to the text you heard. Also check it carefully for grammatical mistakes.

Step 2

T : Now, let's rewrite the text. First, in groups of three, put together all the words that each member heard. Then, working in your group, try to make sentences with those words. And then compare your group's sentences with other groups' sentences. Using all the sentences available, rewrite the text. And check it to make sure the meaning is similar to the text I read.

Step 3

T : Now, I'll pass out the original text that I read to you. Compare your group's text with the original one. How is the original different from yours? Look at both content and passive forms. And then make a presentation about the differences you've found between the two texts.

Step 3

T : Now, I will give you the original text. On the text, I've already underlined some parts. [Only the passive forms in the text are underlined.] Mark the parts in your group's text that you think match those underlined parts. Make your group's text as similar as possible to the original text.

The lesson plans are for the second class period. In the first class period, students learned how passive sentences are formed. One of the aims of today's class is to help the students learn when passives are preferred to their corresponding active sentences.

4 Teacher Talk Modification

(1) Purpose

The purpose of teacher talk modification is to <u>make spoken language more accessible and understandable for students</u>, especially in language learning or content-based instruction. It involves adjusting how teachers speak to support student comprehension and engagement.

(2) Main Reasons for Modifying Teacher Talk

① Enhance Comprehension

- Simplifying vocabulary, sentence structure, and speaking rate helps students grasp the content more easily: lexical modification & syntactic modification
- Rephrasing or repeating key ideas reinforces understanding.

② Support Language Acquisition

By providing input that's just above students' current level (i.e., comprehensible input), teachers help learners gradually acquire new language.

③ Maintain Student Engagement

Clear and adapted language keeps students focused and encourages participation.

④ Model Appropriate Language Use

Teachers can demonstrate correct grammar, pronunciation, and usage in ways that are easier for learners to notice and imitate.

⑤ Facilitate Classroom Management

Using clear, concise instructions and predictable routines reduces confusion and helps maintain order.

In short, teacher talk modification bridges the gap between teacher input and student understanding, making teaching more effective, especially for diverse learners or second language learners.

(3) Types

① Simplification: lexical and syntactic modifications

- Definition: Using simpler vocabulary and grammar structures when explaining.
- Example: Instead of saying, "The present perfect is used to denote actions that have occurred at an unspecified time," a teacher might say, "We use the present perfect when we don't say exactly when something happened."

② Slowing Down Speech

- Definition: Speaking at a slower pace to give students time to process language.
- Example: Slowing down when explaining verb forms like "has eaten," "have gone," to allow learners to catch the form and meaning.

③ Repetition and Paraphrasing

- Definition: Repeating key grammar points or rephrasing them in different ways.
- Example: "He has eaten breakfast. That means he finished eating. It's done. He's not eating now."

④ Use of Gestures and Visuals

- Definition: Supporting explanations with hand gestures, drawings, or realia.
- Example: Pointing backward over the shoulder to signal "past," or using a timeline to show how tenses differ.

⑤ Use of Examples and Modeling

- Definition: Providing multiple, clear examples of the grammar in context.
- Example: Giving several sentences using the target structure.
  She has gone to the store.
  They have visited Japan.
  We have finished our homework.

⑥ Use of Checking Questions (Concept Checking Questions-CCQs)

- Definition: Asking simple questions to confirm understanding of a grammar rule.
- Example: After teaching the past perfect.
  "Did it happen before or after the other action?"
  "Was it finished before the story?"

⑦ Reduction of Idiomatic or Complex Expressions

- Definition: Avoiding idioms, slang, or culturally loaded expressions during grammar explanations.
- Example: Instead of saying "That's old hat," just say "That's something people have known for a long time."

These modifications help learners notice and understand grammar patterns more easily, making instruction more effective and learner-centered.

5 Task difficulty

말하기 활동의 난이도와 관련하여 교사가 고려해야 하는 세 가지 요소는 자료, 과업 그리고 학습자 요인이다.

Text	• How dense/complex are the texts that learners are required to process? • How abstract/concrete is the content in relation to the learners experience? How much contextual support is provided?
Task	• How many steps are involved in the task? • How relevant and meaningful is the task? • How much time is available? • What degree of grammatical accuracy is provided? • How much practice or rehearsal time is available?
Learner	• The level of confidence • Motivation of learners • Prior knowledge of content • Degree of linguistic knowledge • Skill, extent of cultural knowledge • Degree of familiarity with task type itself

NEW

Build Up

박현수 영어교육론 Ⅲ-1 기출문제

Guideline for Pre-service Teachers
주제별 기출분석 정리

초판인쇄 | 2025. 5. 2. **초판발행** | 2025. 5. 9. **편저자** | 박현수

발행인 | 박 용 **발행처** | (주)박문각출판 **표지디자인** | 박문각 디자인팀

등록 | 2015년 4월 29일 제2019-000137호

주소 | 06654 서울시 서초구 효령로 283 서경빌딩 **팩스** | (02)584-2927

전화 | 교재주문·학습문의 (02)6466-7202

정가 27,000원(1, 2권 포함)
ISBN 979-11-7262-793-5 | ISBN 979-11-7262-792-8(세트)